The Power of Religion / Religion and Power

European Academy of Religion (EuARe) Lectures

EuARe Executive Committee:
Karla Boersma, Francesca Cadeddu, Jocelyne Cesari,
Silvio Ferrari, Vincente Fortier, Hans-Peter Grosshans,
Pantelis Kalaitzidis, Frederik Pedersen,
Herman J. Selderhuis

Volume 3

The Power of Religion / Religion and Power

Third Annual Conference 2020

Edited by
Herman J. Selderhuis

DE GRUYTER

Published with the support of the Policy Planning Unit of the Italian Ministry of Foreign Affairs and the International Cooperation (under Article 23-bis of DPR 18/1967). The opinions expressed are those of the authors. They do not reflect the opinions or views of FSCIRE or the Italian Ministry of Foreign Affairs and International Cooperation.

www.europeanacademyofreligion.org
in cooperation with

Ministero degli Affari Esteri
e della Cooperazione Internazionale

MINISTERO DELL'ISTRUZIONE DELL'UNIVERSITA' E DELLA RICERCA

Opera realizzata con il supporto di

ISBN 978-3-11-122805-1
e-ISBN (PDF) 978-3-11-122910-2
e-ISBN (EPUB) 978-3-11-123000-9
DOI https://doi.org/10.1515/9783111229102
ISSN 2940-455X

This work is licensed under the Creative Commons Attribution 4.0 International License.
For details go to https://creativecommons.org/licenses/by/4.0/.

Library of Congress Control Number: 2023902387

Bibliographic information published by the Deutsche Nationalbibliothek
The Deutsche Nationalbibliothek lists this publication in the Deutsche Nationalbibliografie; detailed bibliographic data are available on the Internet at http://dnb.dnb.de.

© 2023 with the author(s), editing © Herman J. Selderhuis, published by Walter de Gruyter GmbH, Berlin/Boston. This book is published with open access at www.degruyter.com.
Printing and binding: CPI books GmbH, Leck

www.degruyter.com

Contents

Herman J. Selderhuis
Introduction —— 1

R. Scott Appleby
Hallowed Be Thy/My Name: Power and Glory in the Extremist Religious Imagination —— 5

Cyril Hovorun
Politicisation of Religion: Eastern Christian Cases —— 17

Susanne Schröter
Islam, Politics, and Society in Germany —— 41

Kristina Stoeckl
Europe's New Religious Conflicts: Russian Orthodoxy, American Christian Conservatives and the Emergence of a European Populist Christian Right-Wing —— 53

Notes on Contributors —— 61

Index of Names —— 63

Herman J. Selderhuis
Introduction

1 The 2020 Conference

In this book readers will find the lectures presented at the conference that did not take place, yet was highly successful. When the Executive Committee of EuARe decided early in 2019 that "The Power of Religion / Religion and Power" would be the leading topic, no-one had the slightest idea that the power of a pandemic would be stronger than our enthusiasm, plans and preparations. After the successful launch of the European Academy of Religion at the Ex Nihilo Conference, held in Bologna from 18 to 22 June 2017, and the two subsequent conferences of 5–8 March 2018 and 4–7 March 2019, both of which also took place in Bologna, we were all looking forward to a future event in that city and to another successful conference. All was set for a meeting with even more participants, sessions, exhibits and events than in the previous years, and we were certainly all looking forward to it as a stimulating place for scholars, projects, ideas and to enjoying the hospitality, the grandeur, the climate and the food and wines of Bologna. This was not to be, but we were able to appreciate all the above in the 2021 conference, which was held in Münster (Germany), and in the following one in 2022, that took place in Bologna again.

Once more, I wish to express my gratitude to our friends at the Fondazione per le scienze religiose in Bologna. The communication and organisation were excellent on this occasion, too, and I regret that they carried out all the preparatory work without being able to share their achievements with us. Our thanks are due to Alberto Melloni and his team for continuing support, for providing us with the joy of cooperation and for preparing this book even under such unusual circumstances.

Yet, as I have already written, the conference was successful since the team at Fscire swiftly shifted to an online programme presenting lectures and panel-sessions that many could enjoy worldwide. Our thanks also go to the presenters and organisers of sessions who were willing to speak and to transmit their knowledge: although communication with the audience was limited, the latest results in religious studies could still be shared and discussed. In this sense, the online 2020 conference was undoubtedly successful and will be so for a long period because in this volume readers will find the complete plenary papers of all the keynote lecturers. The pandemic may be powerful, but the proven power of a book will remain so for many centuries. This is not a large volume, but its content constitutes a great contribution to religious studies and a useful bridge between Bologna 2020 and Münster 2021.

2 The Power of Religion

With the choice of the topic for the 2020 conference, the Executive Committee of EuARe wished to highlight the powerful effect that religion has on public and personal life and that this effect relates to all fields of life, such as fashion, politics, art, leisure, ethics and science. The relevance of the topic is seen in present-day discussions, for example on the effects that religious education at home has on the behaviour of children and young adults in public life, or on national and international developments in which the power that religion exerts on political decisions becomes evident. Considering this from the opposite viewpoint, we also see that politicians are conscious of the power of religion and endeavour to make use of it. This too, however, is not just a recent phenomenon. Throughout the centuries, political powers have exploited religions, religious leaders, religious buildings and religious symbols; furthermore, such powers know that religion itself is more powerful than politics, since it has an immense effect on the heart, the mind and the emotions of people, which is an effect that politics is in no way capable of attaining. The interdisciplinarity that EuARe seeks to stimulate can help to reveal the historical roots of specific relationships between religion and politics besides create an awareness that the power of religion in its relation to political power has played a major role worldwide for centuries. This historical approach can offer insights into patterns and will help to understand today's discussions better.

The relationship between power and religion tends to be seen merely negatively, particularly when it concerns politics, yet history and the present also demonstrate how religion can have a powerful, positive effect on individuals and societies. Religion in itself, especially believers and their religious leaders, have the power to reconcile, to initiate efforts to create or preserve peace and good relations and to encourage through, for example, religious education and preaching, an attitude of mutual understanding. Examples of this can be found throughout history, including more recent history. The fall of the Berlin Wall in 1989 as a symbol of the end of the division between Eastern and Western Europe demonstrated the power of the church and of its believers: it was during the prayer meetings on Monday evening in Leipzig in September 1987 that this wall started to disintegrate, and this occurred in a socialist country where religion had in many respects been highly restricted and where the political party even tried to erase anything pertaining to it.

3 Widespread Power

This book presents an important but as yet still limited part of the broader perspective that the topic opens up; among others, here are just three additional examples of subjects that could be researched through the lens of the power of religion: literature, art and law. As far as literature is concerned, the reference is not just to the powerful influence of religious books, especially of the normative and foundational books of the various religions. What is of interest is how religion had, and has, the power to influence writers in their choice of words, phrases, plots, personalities and settings. The author's personal attitude towards religion is reflected, demonstrating the powerful influence it has exerted on him/her and thereby transmitting a similar effect to the reader. Therefore, many of the great writers and many of the great novels in the history of literature would not have obtained the label 'great' without the power of religion which they experienced. The same is true of art. Granada and Palermo, which are admired by multitudes of tourists and other visitors, are merely two of the European cities that demonstrate the power of Islam on art and architecture. Religious knowledge is necessary to understand and to appreciate these artistic expressions correctly. Medieval Islamic art is thus an excellent example of the constructive and lasting power that religion may have on art, and an example that can counter the idea, fostered by the destructive acts of IS towards cultural heritage, that, Islam and art are categories which can in no way co-exist.

As a third and final example, I wish to mention law. The issue of law and religion is a controversial topic, mainly due to debates on religious laws that conflict with, or threaten, civil law, or, on the contrary, civil law that intrudes upon religious law. This certainly concerns the power, or the lack of power, of religion, yet it is also important and interesting to consider how religion shaped concepts of law that are generally accepted as common or civil law without its being noticed that they have substantial religious foundations. This means that in these cases religion exerts a clear and long-lasting power without being identified as such.

Far more could be said about these three examples, and many others could be mentioned, but I think this is sufficient to see that the 2020 topic is very important not merely for present-day developments in the world but also both for pointing out lacunae in religious studies and for indicating that for the coming decades of EuARe conferences there will be no shortage of themes for lectures, sessions and panels.

4 Agenda

EuAre has no political or religious agenda, only an academic one. Academic, however, does not signify that EuARe operates in an ivory tower, since academics, including those active in religious studies, or, even better, particularly those involved in religious studies, should always have the intention to be of service to the world at large. Research is not effected merely for the sake of further research but for the sake of public well-being. The search for a vaccine to combat the pandemic that prevented us from meeting in Bologna is a clear example of the purpose of research, that is to say, ultimately for the wider public. When the theme of the power of religion is concerned, research can provide better insights into the effects that religion has on roles and relationships within families, as well as between sexes. Thanks to its very nature, research must and does refrain from labelling these effects as either positive or negative, but it may help to understand why and how religion can have the power to cause or counter injustice. Here the power of religious studies comes into view, including the challenge to handle this power in a proper, unbiased, that is scholarly, way. EuARe has started to encourage this outlook, and our agenda reflects the enthusiasm for continuing along this path, in spite of a powerful pandemic, and with a growing number of scholars and institutions working in the field of religious studies.

R. Scott Appleby
Hallowed Be Thy/My Name: Power and Glory in the Extremist Religious Imagination

In the following, I use the terms *God*, the *sacred*, and the *divine* interchangeably, while recognising that such usage is inadequate and inevitably misleading. First, no term or combination of terms is adequate when referring to a reality widely considered to be ineffable – beyond the ability of words to comprehend. Second, I will be drawing on examples from *religions* – another contested term – as different in belief, practice, doctrine and cosmology as Christianity and Hinduism, Judaism and Islam. For Hinduism and other South Asian and Eastern traditions, the term God itself is problematic, and conceptualisations of 'divine agency' deserve the kind of nuanced treatment I cannot provide in this format. Hence the over-reliance in what follows on abstract generalisations.

Historically, actors across a variety of world regions and religious communities have behaved in ways understood as being obedient to divine commands, reflecting and celebrating divine glory, or even partaking in divine power. By performing certain prescribed rites, enacting certain ethical imperatives, fulfilling certain perceived obligations, the community or the individual has "given glory and praise to God".

The religious acts warranted by, or expressive of, divine power and glory range from the communal or individual recitation of prayers, to the ritual sacrifice of animals (or human beings), to the launching of military or terrorist attacks on the field of battle. Across this behavioural spectrum the holiness and majesty of the sacred is equated with, dependent upon, or manifest by the *power* of the sacred. And in some quarters, as we shall see, the devout have understood divine power as merely the extrapolation of earthly power.

The conflation of godly and human power became particularly pronounced in some quarters during the postcolonial period, as the comprehensive claims of the modern nation-state to absolute sovereignty over its inhabitants were challenged by the rise of extra-state and transnational actors 'from below'. Empowered by communications and arms technologies that helped them overcome their natural disadvantages in the face of massive state power and mobility, these new, subversive religious actors attempted, in their own bid for sovereignty, to accrue the kind of power desired by the modern secular nation-state – namely, the power to comprehend and control the whole of social and personal life. Only the Almighty, they comforted themselves, could bestow that kind of mastery. And so, from the ranks of believers they recruited technocrats, engineers, lawyers, accountants to operationalise their vision of a semi-theocratic order, and from the rootless masses, they enticed gullible young men to provide the muscle.

Subtler and more inclusive notions of what constitutes divine majesty, of how one best serves the glory of God, gained little traction among the militants.

This conflation of the petty machinations of mortals and the awesome grandeur of the sacred is a curious phenomenon requiring explanation.

1 The Dynamics of the Enclave

The new religious subcultures typically begin as enclaves, enclosed spaces surrounded by hostile or threatening territory. Membership in the enclave is voluntary, and the boundaries between insiders and outsiders must be strictly policed. Moral persuasion is used to keep insiders inside; much is made in the enclave of what Emmanuel Sivan calls the "wall of virtue". An enclave's outer boundary is porous, he observes,

> due above all to the material and social temptations of the central community, which enjoys prestige, cultural hegemony, and access to government sanctions as well as to resources (whether the state's or of wealthy individuals). Virtually the only thing the beleaguered enclave can offer from its own authority is moral reward.[1]

Virtue is its own reward, especially when the virtuous believe that their reward will be great in heaven. Sivan continues: "A sort of 'wall of virtue' is thereby constructed, separating the saved, free, equal (before God or before history), and morally superior enclave from the hitherto-tempting central community".[2]

Members of the enclave see themselves as the 'true believers', a phrase militant religious groups use to set themselves in sharp contrast to their co-religionists who are still stuck in the compromised mainstream religious tradition, which has succumbed to the lures of the pluralist, secular, modern world. Denizens of the enclave appropriate the symbols, rituals and lexicon of the larger, historic tradition, which they seek to reform or to supplant. They are "the righteous," "the pure," or "the elect." In their steadfast refusal to capitulate to the priorities of the world, they believe themselves to exalt the sacred, to reflect the glory of God.

The members of the enclave build a religious subculture, a ferocious rival to the mainstream, even as they appropriate traditional terms and concepts. In the Hebrew Bible the word for "glory" carries the simple meaning of heaviness or

---

[1] E. Sivan, "The Enclave Culture", in M.E. Marty/ R.S. Appleby (eds.), *Fundamentalism Comprehended* (vol. 5 of *The Fundamentalism Project*, Chicago/London: University of Chicago Press, 1995), 11–68, on p. 17.
[2] Ibid., 18.

weight. It was used in everyday speech to express the worth of a person in the material sense. Over time, the term came to express the ideas of importance, greatness, honour, splendour and, not least, power. These associations can be found in the French and Latin roots of the term.

Though not included in New Testament accounts of the prayer Jesus taught his followers, the earliest Christians, and many still today, recite the following coda at the end of the Lord's Prayer: "For thine is the kingdom and the power, and the glory, for ever and ever". Indeed, Christian religious language is abounding in reference to the glory, power and might of the Most High. The Gloria, a hymn sung or recited most weeks in Catholic Mass, begins "Glory to God in the highest" and goes on to praise God "for your glory". Countless acts of generosity, love and self-sacrifice, large and small, are dedicated to the glorification of God.

Muslims recite the now well-known and multivalent Arabic phrase *Allahu Akbar* (God is Greater!) in various situations including the *Salah* or obligatory daily prayers; but it has also entered into popular lexicon as a result of being invoked by some extremist Muslims engaged in violent and highly public acts of violence intended either to share in the glory of God or to exalt Allah. The phrase has a unique and complex history beyond its early use and conception; what will concern us here is the transmutation of such traditional and time-honoured paeans to the glory of the Most High, into rallying cries of religious extremists.

What conception of the Divine, then, lies behind this ubiquitous insistence on giving glory to God, on adoring and exalting God's majesty and dominant power? Does the Holy One in some way *need* the praise of his creatures? Or does the significance of attributing power and glory to the sacred lie not in a divine but a very human need? Is the true believer somehow brought to greater depths of fulfilment or to greater heights of holiness by extolling and somehow partaking of the glory and power of the Creator and Redeemer?

2 An Awkward Mimesis of the Secular

These militant expressions of the idea of the power and glory of the sacred, propelled by the social dynamics and structural conditions of late mo dernity, play a central role in the modern religious imaginary. For certain religious subcultures, giving and receiving glory is associated with secular notions of prosperity, honour and success, and with manifestations of power by the modern state. The irony is striking. In an effort to protect religion from the state, the enclave has spawned movements and networks that display an activist, aggressive and militant form of religiosity which, in its ideological traits and organisational dynamics, reflects the merging of mod ern secular and traditionally religious sensibilities, practices and goals.

The emergence and evolution of this religious-secular hybrid yields insights into our major conference theme of religion and power.

One notes in the following summaries of case studies a common theme: originally repelled by and distancing themselves from the compromised and sullied religious mainstream, these supposed rejectionists came to persuade themselves that seeking worldly power was their only option in the effort to preserve doctrinal, ritual and communal purity. They justified this quest for mundane power by an appeal to the glorification of God. However, they selected the more anthropomorphised portrayals of the Holy One with in the multivalent and sometimes self-contradictory texts and myths of their respective traditions. Ignoring the subtler manifestations of divine majesty, however, they failed to heed the scriptural and traditional warnings against conflating God's ways with human ways. Rather, they have engaged in a kind of mimesis (however awkward or incomplete) of the very secular milieu they profess to loathe. Attaining some measure of the powers wielded by the secular state, or manipulating the secular state into doing their bidding, has become a tried-and-true method and a primary benchmark of success.

3 Cases

The emergence of Religious Zionism in Israel during the latter half of the twentieth century illustrates the blending of traditional religious and modern secular notions of power and glory, with its profound implications for religious agency.

As in many other cases, this emergent subgroup was not quite 'traditional'; rather than struggle with the ambiguities and ambivalences that make a religious tradition both vexing and enlivening as an enduring argument about what constitutes the good, the just and the merciful under divine sovereignty, the Jewish 'fundamentalists' leaned heavily on one leg of the ancient wisdom and theodicy and allowed the other to atrophy.

The fear and trembling with which the people of ancient Israel encountered the awesome power of YHWH is on display throughout the Hebrew Bible, most dramatically, perhaps, in the Book of Exodus and the Book of Job, where the gulf between absolute (and occasionally mercurial) divine power, on the one hand, and human frailty, on the other, is vast. Passages in these key texts place on display a dimension of the Deity that appears all too human. The Lord of Moses seems to crave publicity, for example, and can be quite the bully. The English translations of a diverting passage, Exodus 14:4, vary, but in any version the following discourse is striking: "I will harden Pharaoh's heart, and he will pursue them. But I will gain glory for myself over Pharaoh and all his army, and the Egyptians will know that

I am the LORD". Bloody retribution and seemingly arbitrary punishment is not beneath the God of Exodus and Job.³

Equally noteworthy in the Hebrew Bible, and even in these very books, however, are passages that set YHWH's governing presence in contrast to destructive power; compare the passages cited above to those extolling the "gentle whisper" of God (1 Kings 19:12, Job 4:16). Even more prevalent is the insistence that God alone holds the prerogative of divine punishment; vengeance upon his enemies is reserved for the Lord God of Hosts alone, not for humans. (The classic text is Deuteronomy 32:35, but the theme reappears throughout, in Leviticus, Numbers, Proverbs and in other books).

History shows Jewish sages and leaders grappling with these tensions. On the one hand, there is ample scriptural evidence that the Lord authorises iconic figures such as Moses and David to serve his purpos es through miracles, wily calculation and temporal rule; accordingly, biblical-era Judaism developed several political models, including priestly theocracy. Alongside the rise of Jewish councils and other forms of religious and communal self-government during the rabbinic and medieval periods, on the other hand, the political environment dictated, and one sees, a delicate and halting approach to political power and to secular authorities. Indeed, throughout Jewish experience, there is a profound hesitation to connect the dots, that is, to leap to the conclusion that the necessary exercise of Jewish self-governance in this or that dispensation should be taken to correspond in some neat, obvious or linear fashion to God's plan of salvation for the people of Israel.

In the twentieth century, following the Holocaust and the migration to Palestine, as Jews of various stripes were imagining the State of Israel into existence, this vein of trembling and fear before the transcendent power and inscrutable purposes of the Lord resurfaced in the modern Haredi movement. The Haredim rejected and denounced secular Zionist pretensions to establish an authentically Jewish state, and withdrew into enclaves dedicated to awaiting the arrival of the Messiah.⁴

In the 1960s, emerging fully in the 1970s in the wake of the near-disastrous Yom Kippur War, however, an aggressive, confident, militant band of Religious Zionists –

---

3 The medieval rabbinic commentator, Rashi, expounds: "When the Holy One, blessed be God, takes vengeance on the wicked, God's name is magnified and honored. And, similarly, Scripture says (Ezek 38:22–23); 'I will punish him with pestilence and with bloodshed. [...] Thus I will manifest My greatness and My holiness, and make Myself known in the sight of many Nations. And they shall know that I am the Eternal"; quoted in A. Grossman, *Rashi* (Portland, OR: Littman Library of Jewish Civilization, 2012).
4 M. Friedman/S.C. Heilman, "Religious Fundamentalism and Religious Jews: The Case of the Haredim", in M.E. Marty/R.S. Appleby (ed.), *Fundamentalisms Observed* (Chicago: University of Chicago Press, 1991), 197–264.

the Gush Emunim or Bloc of the Faithful – became convinced that the founding and survival of the State of Israel was prominent among the signs of the advent of the Messianic era. By means of their illegal settlements in territories occupied by Israel after the Six-Day War of 1967 and their provocations of both Palestinian Arabs and the political leaders of the Israeli state, they sought not only to hasten but also to implement the divine plan.

The movement enjoyed initial success in luring the Israeli government to consolidate its extra-legal incursions and to build state-funded settlements as part of a plan to expand the borders of the State of Israel. Gush Emunim dreamed of an expansion to encompass the biblical Whole Land of Israel, "from the Nile to the Euphrates". The movement is a hybrid. Its early core included both graduates of the Mercaz HaRav (The Central Universal Yeshiva) who were disciples of Rabbi Kook, and also secular activists hailing from previous land expansion campaigns. The operational wing of the movement placed modern communications technology and organisational design at the service of irredentist Messianism; underground elements studied and adopted modern terrorist tactics.[5] Over time Gush Emunim was 'domesticated', with some of its early members serving in the Knesset and eventually becoming assimilated into the Israeli political establishment.

Known today as "Ne'emanei Eretz Yisrael" ("those who are faithful to the Land of Israel"), the Gush Emunim, by one view, is a member of a global 'family' of modern religious nationalisms. Religious nationalists of our day exceed the limits of mundane ultra-nationalism in two ways. First, they explicitly present the nation as sacred or as partaking of the sacred. Here the discourse of divine power and glory is pervasive. Second, the overt sacralisation of the nation is embraced by religious nationalists, such as the Gush or the Hindutva ('Hinduness') movement in India, as a vital step toward realising the fulfillment of the religion itself – Judaism, in the former case, Hinduism in the latter.

In virtually all the major religious traditions in the past several decades, one can document a tendency towards what we might call the temporising of divine power and its replacement by decidedly human empire-building.

Christianity is certainly no exception; examples are ubiquitous. Globe-spanning Pentecostalism promises its hundreds of millions of adherents healing and material as well as spiritual prosperity; one variant is known as the "name-it-and-claim it gospel". Although local and national Pentecostal churches reflect their disparate cultural settings, there is a certain quasi-corporate template, one might say, that lends a certain homogeneity to the mega-churches, wherever they are situated.

---

5 See G. Aran, "Jewish Zionist Fundamentalism: The Bloc of the Faithful in Israel (Gush Emunim)", in ibid., 265–344.

Affiliated with the World Assemblies of God, the Yoido Full Gospel Church of Seoul, South Korea, founded in 1958, boasts 480,000 members, making it one of the largest single churches on the planet. Despite its distinctive aspects, Yoido preaches the necessity of a born-again experience and regeneration by the Holy Spirit, which is marked by speaking in tongues and divinely inspired preaching, witnessing, healing of the sick and protection from sickness. While these are spiritual gifts described and promised in the New Testament, Pentecostal churches are not apolitical, as is sometimes claimed. Rather, they have supported state or municipal politicians, including authoritarian leaders in Latin America and elsewhere, whose policies have cleared the way for church proselytism and expansion.[6]

Even once-quietist, separatist Christian fundamentalists have been drawn into the political power game. "While the Lord tarries" was a favoured locution of Bob Jones, Jr, the second president and chancellor of Bob Jones University, the Christian fundamentalist university in Greenville, South Carolina. Jones recited this phrase regularly to explain and justify why he and other Christian pastors had vowed not to wait upon the vengeance of the Lord, but to fight back against the twentieth century onset of a hegemonic godless culture desacralising American institutions at the behest of an aggressive secular state. Put simply: the Lord was tarrying, postponing his prophesied and long anticipated return to Earth in power and glory, and so the devout Christian must clear the threshing floor, create the social and political conditions that would, as it were, lure the Lord into fulfilling his promise of a triumphant return marked by a righteous display of purifying power.

These millennialist imaginings have their dark side. Whether the triumphant Second Coming of Christ would usher in the End Times prophesied in the Bible (*pre*millennialism) or cap the thousand years of Christ's reign (*post*millennialism), only the born-again believer would escape the withering judgment of the Lord. Hal Lindsey's *The Late Great Planet Earth*,[7] the bestselling nonfiction book of the 1970s in America, popularised this apocalyptic fever-dream, according to which current events (e.g., the establishment of the State of Israel and the subsequent expansion of its geographical borders) presaged the rapture of fundamental Christians directly into heaven before the rise of the satanic Antichrist. Twenty-five years later Tim LaHaye and Jerry B. Jenkins launched a series of sixteen bestselling Christian novels (published between 1995 and 2007, 60 million copies sold worldwide), setting forth in elaborate and bloody detail the tribulations endured by those remaining on earth after the rapture (the Left Behind series, as it is known). The

---

6 See D. Stoll, *Is Latin America Turning Protestant? The Politics of Evangelical Growth* (Berkley, CA: University of California Press, 1991).
7 H. Lindsey, *The Late Great Planet Earth, with C.C. Carlson* (Grand Rapids, MI: Zondervan, 1970).

series imagines an underground network of converts waging a violent campaign against the (secular-liberal-Jewish) "Global Community" – which is eventually annihilated by an avenging Jesus, returning on clouds of glory, death rays emanating from his visage.

For our purposes, what is noteworthy in this fabulous tale and its variants, is the necessary, if not sufficient, role of the true believers in the unfolding of God's glorious victory. They are not merely passive, awaiting on the tarrying Lord to return; rather, they hasten his coming by their strenuous efforts to spread the gospel and to fight back against the godless. As scholars of late modern Christian eschatology have noted, from the 1960s onward there is a drift toward a kind of *post*millennialist activism: the decisive manifestation of divine power and glory is in some way dependent upon the efforts of the believing community on earth.[8]

Indeed, in building a robust and sprawling religious subculture in the United States, the fundamentalists used various tactics, but strict separatism – withdrawal from the fray, leaving the end times to God, letting God be God – faded as a viable option.

Evidence of a similar narrowing of the religious imagination is found, *mutatis mutandis*, among modern Hindu, Roman Catholic and Islamic subcommunities as well. Taking a page from the British colonisers, the members of India's contemporary Hindutva movement reify the sprawling and disparate practices of the Indus valley region as a religion – called Hinduism – in order to lend plausibility to their portrayal of polyglot, religiously plural India as "a Hindu nation." This dual move – sacralising the nation, and glorifying it as the cornerstone or summit of 'orthodox' or 'orthoprax' religion – lends a transcendent or metaphysical depth to exclusionary social norms and discriminatory politics that mere irredentism or 'politics as usual' could not provide. The nation is absolute because it partakes of the sacred; the sacred is bound up in the destiny of the nation.

In his study of Hindus and Muslims in late twentieth century India, Peter van der Veer writes:

> In the construction of the Muslim "other" by Hindu nationalist movements, Muslims are always referred to as a dangerous "foreign element", as not truly Indian. [...] Control over sacred centers [of the nation] and ritual sites is not only crucial to the power of religious elites but is a source of continuous struggle between religious movements [...] The problem [facing

---

[8] See M. Barkun, *A Culture of Conspiracy: Apocalyptic Visions in Contemporary America* (Berkley, CA: University of California Press, 2003); M. Lienesch, *Redeeming America: Piety and Politics in the New Christian Right* (Chapel Hill, NC: University of North Carolina Press, 1993).

secular political leaders] is the state's diminishing capability to arbitrate conflicts [...] in a society characterized by a plurality of cultures.[9]

One can readily see how the definition of the nation as co-terminus with the history and prerogatives of a particular ethno-religious and racial subset of the population is abetted by the construction of that subset as the original 'chosen people'. The politics of exclusion fed by radical populism and right-wing nationalism becomes ever more powerful, then, when minorities are depicted as displacing the rightful heirs of the sacred trust and are thereby easily demonised, not merely as aliens, foreigners and outsiders, but as impure and somehow less than fully human – and, therefore, presented as justifiable targets of violence and other forms of coercion – violence which, in the eyes of the Hindu soldiers, gives glory to the Hindu Lord Ram.

Until fairly recently, the doctrine of the transcendent sovereignty of God shaped mainstream currents within Judaism, Sunni Islam and Protestant Christianity; each in their own ways, these communities honoured the vast gulf between the absolute power of God, and the feeble striving of the sinful or disobedient human subject. In the late modern milieu, as we have seen, however, these religious communities have eroded the imagined distance between Divine sovereignty and "redemptive" human agency.

Meanwhile, for Roman Catholics, Shiʻa Muslims and Hindus, the boundaries between human and divine agency were always more porous. The analogical imagination of Catholicism, for example, authorises forms of *imitatio Christi*. Ayatollahs are themselves "sources of imitation" in the Shiʻa imaginary.

According to this shared family resemblance, or common general perspective on the sacred, saints, martyrs, and other religious virtuosi are believed to be participants in the divine drama, partakers of divine glory, avatars of the transcendent. When the metaphor became military, they were soldiers of Christ, the vanguard of Allah, volunteers to the cause of the Lord Ram. The theological distance to travel between divine glory and earthly striving was not quite as forbidding in these traditions of the 'analogical imagination'. Now they have been joined in their assumed proximity to the divine power by the once "God-fearing" Protestants, Sunnis and Jews.

---

[9] P. Van der Veer, *Religious Nationalism: Hindus and Muslims in India* (Berkley, CA: University of California Press, 1994), 184.

4 A Narrowing of Viable Options?

The question is whether the diversity of religious worldviews and behaviours across and within religious communities has collapsed under the pressure of late modernity. It may well be that separatism, a quietist withdrawal from political belligerence, is simply no longer an option available to modern religious actors who feel increasingly besieged by the encroachments of an undiluted, state-sponsored secularism abetted by rapid communications, digitised global markets and international travel. This certainly seemed to be the conclusion of the Shi'ite followers of the Ayatollah Khomeini, who chose revolution after casting off a closely observed tradition of political quietism observed during the long centuries while the Hidden Imam tarried.[10]

The strategy of the Iranian revolutionaries, the Israeli Jewish settlers, the Christian fundamentalists, the Hindu nationalists, seems to be: if you cannot beat secularism, then dilute it, join it, so to speak, but in so doing, refine it, turn it to religious ends.

By way of consequences, divine majesty and the power emanating therefrom is now placed at the service of identifying, protecting and militarising the elect, the chosen ones, the elite spiritual vanguard – and of the casting of all others into the fire. This is the way to glorify God. In this aspiration in itself, there is nothing new or modern. But I want to call attention to the specific ironies, reversals and unintended outcomes incumbent on those who have chosen to evoke ancient hatreds through the means of modern political ideologies and enabling technologies. In short, over the last several generations one can trace a weakening of these historically divergent and heterogeneous Muslim, Hindu, Jewish and Christian theologies, religious anthropologies, practices and worldviews. Within and across multigenerational modern religious communities, indeed, we have seen the rise of an alternative mode of religiosity, labelled variously fundamentalism, ultra-Orthodoxy, or neo-traditionalism.

Whatever we call this ideologically-driven instrumentalisation of the relationship between human agency and divine power, it has reduced this richly allusive mode of religious imagination to the merely mundane or secular imperatives of narrow political theology. Meanwhile, the separatist option, a withdrawing from political action into the domain of prayer and community-building, which had for-

---

10 See S.A. Arjomand, "Axial civilizations, multiple modernities, and Islam", *Journal of Classical Sociology* 11/33 (2011): 327–335; and S.A. Arjomand, *The Turban for the Crown: The Islamic revolution in Iran* (New York, NY: Oxford University Press, 1988); J. Cole, *Sacred Space and Holy War: The Politics, Culture and History of Shiite Islam* (London: I.B. Tauris, 2002).

merly been authorised by the *via negativa* – God is nothing like man, and so man must fall on his knees in supplication and obedience – has become increasingly difficult to realise in a world bent on encroaching upon every sacred haven or enclave.

Rabbi Haym Soloveitchik has written eloquently of the transformation of the twentieth-century Jewish community,

> Under the pressure of a nascent Jewish variant on fundmentalism, which displaced the authority of the family and local community in favour of the overweening rabbinic and scholarly policing of conformity to newly set orthodox standards, instructive texts upon texts, laws and behavioural codes. Soloveitchik describes it as a shift from a culture of mimesis to a culture of performance. And in the shift, the fear of God was lost, replaced by the fear of the rabbi.[11]

Such depredations have occurred under the pressure of modern secular ideologies and late modern processes of hybridisation and politicisation. Contemporary and recent reformist, revolutionary, fundamentalist and other politicised social movements have emerged in the context of hyper-modernity, an era characterised by unprecedented globalising trends, ideologies of nationalism and the omnipresent totalising nation-state. In this milieu, religion is seldom the sole player, and religious actors themselves are susceptible to worldviews and habits of mind embedded in structures and processes derived not from religious but from worldly (i.e. secular) trajectories.

Accordingly, innumerable books and articles published over the last few decades modify the category religious violence by embedding religious agency within encompassing nationalist and ethnic narratives. Such ethno-religious and ethno-nationalist modes of religious agency are examples of 'weak religion', in that longstanding religious motivations and dynamics have been hijacked by violence-prone extremist actors and subordinated to state or other secular agendas. The dependent role of religious actors, whether those who must co-exist with secularists within a mixed movement, or those with mixed motives themselves, reflects the vulnerability of religious leaders and institutions to the manipulations of state, nationalist and ethnic forces in their societies. The religious element, that is to say, is relatively weak.[12]

---

11 H. Soloveitchik, "Migration, Acculturation and the New Role of Texts in the Haredi World", in M.E. Marty/R.S. Appleby (ed.), *Accounting for Fundamentalisms: The Dynamic Character of Movements* (Chicago: University of Chicago Press, 1994), 197–235.
12 R.S. Appleby, "Religious Violence: The Strong, the Weak, and the Pathological", in A. Omer/R.S. Appleby/D. Little (ed.), *The Oxford Handbook of Religion, Conflict, and Peacebuilding* (New York, NY: Oxford University Press, 2015), 183–211.

A largely overlooked dimension of this pattern of sanctification and deepening of secular trends is the way giving glory to God has been reinterpreted by modern religious actors. The wielding of shabby worldly power now appears as central to the fulfilment of this obligation. In this context, the lived meaning of power and of glory is woefully truncated. Demographically, alas, it is now the tentative, the religious who prefer to worship God via a quiet whisper, rather than to enact the divine glory themselves, who seem the remnant.

Cyril Hovorun
Politicisation of Religion: Eastern Christian Cases

In this chapter I shall address the issue of religion being politicised. This issue has been well-studied in the West, but is almost ignored by scholarship in the East. At the same time, the Eastern patterns of politicised religion are prototypes of many Western patterns. In looking at the Eastern cases of politicised religion, I am going to utilise both a microscope and a telescope, first drawing your attention to smaller cases, which will then reveal larger panoramic vistas.

1 Political Theology

Let me start with the discussion of the term *political theology*, which took place in interwar Germany between two conservative Catholic[1] soulmates, Carl Schmitt and Erik Peterson. Schmitt re-coined the term political theology, which he, as a scholar of ancient Roman law, may have borrowed from Marcus Terentius Varro, who used it in a different context.[2] Thanks to this re-coinage, Schmitt is sometimes called the godfather of political theology.[3] Of course, he was not. There were many political theologies before him, even though they were not called political theologies. Schmitt used this catchphrase to explain his own theory of state. His concern was to identify the sources of legitimacy for laws. He believed that the state itself cannot be a source of its legal order.[4] This order emerges ex nihilo, as it were. The initial legal order, according to Schmitt, is the result of a 'miracle', which happens in the 'situation of emergency'. The source of this order cannot be truth or nature, but the authority personified. This train of thought proved useful for Adolf Hitler, who was looking for the legal means of overcoming the crisis of the Weimar constitutional order. Schmitt identified this crisis as a situation of emergency, which can be solved with the law personified. Thus he established that a given political leader who per-

---

[1] Peterson converted from Lutheranism under the influence of Schmitt.
[2] According to Augustine, Varro spoke of the Stoic theology, which consisted of a political theology as juxtaposed to the mythical and cosmological theologies (*De civitate Dei* 4.27, 31).
[3] See M. Kirwan, *Political Theology: An Introduction* (Minneapolis, MN: Fortress Press, 2009), 26.
[4] He claimed that "the state is neither the creator, nor the source of the legal order"; see C. Schmitt, *Political Theology: Four Chapters on the Concept of Sovereignty* (Cambridge, MA: MIT Press, 1985), 19.

Open Access. © 2023 Cyril Hovorun, published by De Gruyter. This work is licensed under the Creative Commons Attribution 4.0 International License.
https://doi.org/10.1515/9783111229102-003

sonifies law is one who may override the existing constitutional norms. The führer had his eureka moment.

Schmitt provided a theoretical framework for Hitler's rise to power. As the President of the National Socialist Association of German Legal Professionals, he came to be the 'Crown Jurist' of National Socialism. From justifying the extraordinary authority of the führer, Schmitt evolved to defending extra-judicial killings of Hitler's political opponents and excluding Jews from German jurisprudence. After the war he was tried at Nuremberg and was prohibited to teach in German universities (most professors who collaborated with Nazis were allowed to teach, regardless of denazification). He continued to be an influential public intellectual, with strong conservative views, until his death in 1985.

The concept of political theology was crucial for Schmitt, because it helped him explain and reshape the established legal institutions by the instruments transcendent to law. He chose theology to be such an instrument, and famously claimed that "all significant concepts of the modern theory of the state are secularised theological concepts".[5] In other words, as György Geréby has put it, "the conceptual framework of a world, even if deprived of the divine, still shows a 'theological' structure".[6] Many modern scholars would concur with this point of Schmitt's.[7]

However, Erik Peterson, once a friend of Carl Schmitt, disagreed. He noted how Schmitt had utilised his concept of political theology to justify the Nazi regime, and sounded the alarm. However, Peterson objected not only to one particular ramification of political theology, but to the concept *per se*. In his argumentation, he used a particular case, which, he believed, would demonstrate that the entire method of analogy between the theological and political does not work. This was the case of theological monotheism being projected onto political monarchy in the period of Christian Antiquity.

---

5 Ibid., 36.
6 G. Geréby, "Political Theology Versus Theological Politics: Erik Peterson and Carl Schmitt", *New German Critique* 35/3 (2008), 7–33, on p. 11.
7 A good example could be a conversation between José Casanova, Michael J. Kessler, John Milbank and Mark Lilla, which took place in October 2008 at the Berkley Center for Religion, Peace, and World Affairs at Georgetown University and was then published in the collection *Political Theology for a Plural Age*. All the participants, despite their own disagreements, agreed that Schmitt was wrong in pursuing a political theology that justified Nazism, but he was right in pointing out the theological backdrop of political ideas. Lilla summarised this agreement in the following statement: "Most societies in most times and places have legitimated public authority by some sort of appeal to revelation loosely conceived"; cited in M.J. Kessler (ed.), *Political Theology for a Plural Age* (Oxford: Oxford University Press, 2013), 17.

2 Theological Models for Political Ideologies

Peterson focused on this case in his monograph *Der Monotheismus als politisches Problem* where he argued that the Triune God cannot be a model for political monarchy. The divine Trinity presupposes sharing power, and not its usurpation by one person. Therefore, monarchs, whether they are emperors, kings, presidents or the führer, cannot refer to the Christian God in claiming legitimacy for their power. As Peterson wrote, "with the development of the orthodox dogma [here he means the homoousian interpretation of the Trinity], the idea of divine monarchy loses its political-theological character".[8]

Peterson was not the first theologian to draw parallels between Christian monotheism and political ideologies. Liberal Anglicans tried to justify their 'Christian Socialism' as early as the beginning of the twentieth century. The founder of the British Socialist Party and simultaneously a vicar of the Church of England, also known as the Red Vicar, Conrad Noel, believed that in the Arian controversies,

> The principle at stake, politically, was Democracy *versus* Imperialism; for the Arians held that God was a solitary being remote from the interests of men, a somber emperor in the Heavens, who had not been able to bridge the gulf between the heavens and the earth. Now, if this was so, they argued that such a solitary being was best represented upon earth by a solitary tyrant.[9]

The response of the Nicaean theologians to this belief was that "the highest form of unity which could be conceived by us was the collective unity of the many and the one".[10]

Peterson may have had in mind these discussions about Christian Socialism earlier in the century. He was certainly mindful of patristic insights. A key patristic text for him was an excerpt from the *Third Theological Oration* by Gregory of Nazianzus. According to Gregory, there are three basic ideas about God: anarchy, polyarchy, and monarchy. The former two are pagan and unacceptable for Christians. From the Christian perspective, only monarchy can be accepted. However, this kind of monarchy is not singular and personal, but natural and shared. It is a result of the complete coherence of the divine persons, who share one will and activity:

---

8 E. Peterson, *Der Monotheismus als politisches Problem: ein Beitrag zur Geschichte der politischen Theologie im Imperium Romanum* (Leipzig: Hegner, 1935), 102, cited in Geréby, "Political Theology", 16.
9 C. Noel, *Socialism and Church Tradition* (London: Clarion Press, 1900), 7–8.
10 Ibid.

> We most respect monarchy. However, this is not a monarchy, which is defined by one person, [...] but the [monarchy], which is set together (συνίστησι) by the single honour of the nature, coherence of knowledge, identical movement, and the convergence towards one of those who are from [this one].[11]

Gregory uses the verb συνίστησι, which, because of the prefix συν-, implies that the divine monarchy is composed, not singular. This is a way to say that it is shared. This kind of shared monarchy is possible only for God, but not for any human institution ("created nature", as Gregory puts it).[12] This is because the degree of the divine integrity is unachievable by humans. A political monarchy, which is based on personality, i.e. the absolutist personal power, would fail to demonstrate coherence and integrity. Gregory remarks that such personal power necessarily incurs opposition from many.[13] Only shared power, exercised in coherence, can produce harmony and unity. On the basis of this statement, Peterson concluded that the monarchy of the Christian God cannot be projected onto the monarchy of political rulers, including the führer.

It would not be an exaggeration to say that Peterson utilised the text from Gregory of Nazianzus to polemicise against Nazism in general, and the Schmittean political theology in particular. His study was a metaphor or coded message to communicate to Schmitt his concerns. In a footnote to his study he hinted how "blind and unforseeing" Cicero was, in helping Augustus against Antony, because eventually this contributed to the dictatorship of the former. Jacob Taubes explained this metaphor in his letter to Schmitt: "That *caecus atque improvidus futurorum* was a coded warning directed at you – but you didn't get it".[14]

Peterson was wrong to condemn political theology as such, but he was right to condemn political speculations based on Christian theology,[15] – or what we can more accurately render as the politicisation of religion. What Peterson had in mind was better articulated by his younger contemporary Raymond Aron, who coined the term *religion séculière*. The primary focus of Aron's critique was Marxism and its incarnation in the system of global Communism[16] but he also expanded the category of secular religion to Nazism. In his article "L'avenir des religions séculières",

---

11 *De filio*, Or. 29.2:6–10, cited in J. Barbel, *Gregor von Nazianz: Die fünf theologischen Reden* (Düsseldorf: Patmos, 1963). My translation.
12 *De filio*, Or. 29.2:10, cited in Barbel, *Gregor von Nazianz*.
13 *De filio*, Or. 29.2:7–8, cited in Barbel, *Gregor von Nazianz*.
14 J. Taubes, *Ad Carl Schmitt: Gegenstrebige Fügung* (Berlin: Merve, 1987), 40.
15 See G. Dagron, *Emperor and Priest: The Imperial Office in Byzantium* (Cambridge: Cambridge University Press, 2003), 287.
16 See R. Aron, *The Opium of the Intellectuals* (New York: Norton, 1962).

first published in 1944, he argued that both Communism and Nazism "reproduce certain distinctive characteristics of ancient dogmas. They too offer a global interpretation of the world".[17] This interpretation is divisive. It ontologises evil by incarnating it in large social groups, who are to be contained or exterminated. "Eager to federate hatreds, convinced that humans are drawn together more by hostile emotions than by common affections, they [Communism and Nazism] never rest from displaying to their followers new Bastilles to storm".[18]

Quite unexpectedly, Aron's choice of words was criticised by Hannah Arendt. In her article "Religion and Politics", published in 1953,[19] she addressed her critique mostly to Jules Monnerot, but implicitly also to Raymond Aron. Arendt found any parallel between totalitarian ideologies and religion inappropriate, even blasphemous.[20] She argued that the very nature of Christianity is to be a-political: "The freedom which Christianity brought into the world was a freedom *from* politics".[21] However, the kind of religion that Aron described, just as the kind of theology that Peterson criticised, was not religion or theology in the proper sense.

3 Legitimacy for Christian Emperors

Carl Schmitt was right that the main goal of political theology is to enhance the legitimacy of political regimes. Long before him, in the early fourth century, Eusebius of Caesarea dealt with the legitimacy of the Roman imperial power after this power had legalised Christianity. Before Constantine (sole ruler 324–337), the Roman Empire and the Christian Church treated each other as irreconcilable enemies. The empire attempted to contain, even to extinguish, the church, while the church impatiently waited for the Kingdom of God to replace the kingdom of Caesar.

After Constantine procured a truce with Christianity, legalised its status, and lifted all restrictions that had been imposed upon the church by his predecessors, the empire in return awaited from the church new arguments in support of its own

---

17 R. Aron, "L'avenir des religions séculières", *Commentaire* 8/28–29 (1985), special issue *Raymond Aron, 1905–1983. Histoire et politique: textes et témoignages*, 369–383, on p. 370.
18 Ibid., 374.
19 The article was originally delivered as a paper at a conference in Harvard and then published in 1953 in the Harvard-based journal *Confluence*, edited by Henry Kissinger. It is included in the collection of Arendt's articles, see Hannah Arendt, "Religion and Politics", in Hannah Arendt, *Essays in Understanding, 1930–1954: Formation, Exile, and Totalitarism*, ed. J. Kohn (New York: Harcourt Brace & Co, 1993), 368–390.
20 Arendt, "Religion and Politics", 379.
21 Ibid., 373. Italics original.

legitimacy. Previously, maintaining this legitimacy was a sacred duty of the Greco-Roman public religion. Now a similar service was expected from the Christian Church. Eusebius was among those who sensed the new expectations, and with them new opportunities for the church. In his bulky corpus of writings, he effectively designed a new legitimacy for the old empire. Eusebius, thus, and not Carl Schmitt, should be celebrated as the father of Christian political theology.

Eusebius borrowed two beliefs most valuable for Christians in the pre-Constantinian era and transformed them into two pillars of his political theology. The first was respect to martyrs. Martyrs died, because they were persecuted by the murderous empire. They were literally 'witnesses' of faith and of the injustices that the Roman state imposed upon the Christian Church. Eusebius forged from high respect to martyrs a story in which the presumably 'new' empire substituted the 'old' one, when Constantine ceased persecutions of the church. Martyrdom was merely the rising action in the structure of Eusebius's narrative. Its true climax was the reign of Constantine – the liberator of the church, who opened doors to a new era.

This new era constituted the second pillar of Eusebius's political theology. Albeit with somehow declining vigour, Christians by the time of Eusebius still believed that the Kingdom of God was imminent and that it was a matter of years, not centuries, until the time when Christ would return. Eusebius transformed these eschatological expectations to a new legitimacy for the Roman Empire. After it stopped killing Christians, this empire turned into the millennial kingdom that the Christians had been awaiting since apostolic times. The urge of Eusebius was simple: open your eyes – the Kingdom of God is not coming but has already come. Eusebius's political theology was millennialist: the archenemy of Christianity, the Roman Empire, had become the Kingdom of God. True, it was not yet a full embodiment of this kingdom, but certainly its resemblance. The model suggested by Eusebius was familiar to anyone with an elementary training in Platonism: this world is an imperfect image of the ideal world. It seems that many Christians, particularly those who had recently converted from the educated classes of the Greco-Roman society, began to accept Eusebius's model. At the same time, one cannot imagine a more convincing idea to substantiate the legitimacy of the Roman emperors in the eyes of all their Christian subjects.

We know from modern scholarship that the early church did not focus on persecutions and martyrdom as much as Eusebius imagined, and Constantine did not want to rule the Kingdom of God on earth. He probably did not even intend to change the socio-political structures of the empire he ruled. He simply wanted an extra layer of legitimacy for his rule, in addition to the extant ones, such as, for instance, his pagan role as *Pontifex Maximus*. Nevertheless, the millennialist utopia designed by Eusebius gradually came to be received by the generations of theologians and politicians that followed. Eusebius's political theology became the mainstream political theory in what we now call Byzantium.

At the core of this theory was the concept of symphony, – an ostensibly harmonious relationship between church and state. This concept of symphony was millennialist and utopian. Although it presupposed that the Roman Empire embodied the Kingdom of God as fully as possible, the reality was different, sometimes quite anti-utopian. Iconoclasm, a case to which I shall later return, was such an anti-utopia. At the same time, it should be said that, even if imperfect, symphony did provide a certain extent of peace and harmony to many phases of the relationship between the church and state in Byzantium. Needless to say, even those periods can hardly be acknowledged as anything close to the Kingdom of God on earth.

The first major and sobering crisis in the relations between the Christian Church and the Roman state occurred during their honeymoon. It is sometimes called Arianism – quite misleadingly. It would better be called a controversy about oneness and plurality in God, with the Council of Nicaea in 325 as its milestone. During this crisis, the Roman state suddenly faced not one, but several partners in the place that was supposed to be occupied by one church. On the one hand, there were supporters of the Alexandrian presbyter Arius, including influential Eastern hierarchs, Eusebius of Nicomedia and Eusebius of Caesarea. On the other hand, there were no-less influential hierarchs, led by two popes: one of Alexandria, Athanasius (several tenures between 328 and 373), and another of Rome, Julius (from 337 to 352).

The state, which initially helped the church to condemn the teaching of Arius at the council in Nicaea, soon changed its mind and favoured those whom the council had condemned or marginalised. After that, for most of the fourth century, most Roman emperors supported the cause of those who doubted or rejected Nicaea. Erik Peterson ingeniously realised that the reasons why the state supported the monarchical theology articulated by Arius and his confederates were not only theological but also political. This theology promoted the personal monarchy of the Father and the hierarchical structure of the Trinity. Both ideas could easily be referred to the absolute power of Christian monarchs. But the idea of the equality of the Father and the Son, which the Nicaean Creed promoted, was hardly compatible with the model of monarchy and hierarchy-based power in the utopian Kingdom of God, which had allegedly been incarnated in the Christianised Roman Empire. At the same time, the monarchical/hierarchical model of the Trinity perfectly suited the political model designed by Eusebius. The same Eusebius, by the way, supported monarchy and hierarchy in God.

During the fourth century, when Trinitarian monarchism/hierarchism dominated the Roman Empire and its church, Christian emperors managed to consolidate political power in their own hands to a greater extent than did even their pagan predecessors on the throne. Paradoxically, the Christianised Roman Empire, which was expected to become less autocratic as a result of the Christian message of humility and service, in reality demonstrated the opposite results. Trinitarian monarchism/hierarchism, I believe, was among the main contributors to its transformation towards autocracy.

For a fairly long time, Trinitarian monarchism/hierarchism was the major supplier of legitimacy for the imperial court. At some point, however, it started to lose its charm. This happened when convincing theological arguments against the monarchical and hierarchical model of the Trinity were elaborated upon, especially by the Cappadocians. As a result of this theological development, the monarchical/hierarchical model turned from legitimising to de-legitimising, and was eventually abandoned. Cappadocian theology, however, could not substitute the monarchical/hierarchical Trinity as the source of legitimacy for the Christian emperors.

A new source for political legitimacy was found in its stead, where no one expected to find it – in neo-Platonism. The original attitude of neo-Platonism towards politics was mainly neutral or negative. It has been characterised as upholding "Plato without politics".[22] Despite its a-political or even anti-political standpoint, neo-Platonism, in its Christianised version, came to be employed heavily as a new supplier of political legitimacy for the court, to the extent that it turned into a durable framework for most later versions of Christian political theology. It began again with Eusebius. In his *Praeparatio Evangelica*, he supported the idea of a Christian polity, which was not dissimilar from the utopian Platonopolis designed two decades earlier by the neo-Platonic Porphyry of Tyre.[23] Unlike the neo-Platonic utopian *polis*, which was never built, Eusebius envisaged the entire empire turning into a Christian Platonopolis. To some extent, this vision was realised.

Ancient neo-Platonism provided a clearer and more convincing link between God and the political ruler than even Carl Schmitt could imagine in the 1920s. Schmitt's link was an iconoclastic and transcendental analogy, while for the Christian political theologians trained in neo-Platonism, the divine and political spheres had a more intrinsic relationship of image and participation. Christian emperors were proclaimed the images of the one God. On the one hand, this seemed like a significant downgrade in comparison to the pagan emperors, who had been venerated as deities. On the other hand, a pagan emperor was a deity among many other gods, while the Christian emperor was the sole image of the one God. Although his

---

[22] D.J. O'Meara, *Platonopolis: Platonic Political Philosophy in Late Antiquity* (Oxford: Oxford University Press, 2003), 4.
[23] See J.M. Schott, "Founding Platonopolis: The Platonic Politeia in Eusebius, Porphyry, and Iamblichus", *Journal of Early Christian Studies* 11/4 (2003): 501–531, on p. 502.

authority was assumed to be reduced in Christianity, in effect it only increased. Another neo-Platonic idea of participation established a more intimate connection between one God and the ruler than in Schmitt's analogy. The analogy presupposes a transcendence of the divine power over any political power, while participation makes the divine power immanent in politics.

Neo-Platonism supplied Christianity with an even more politically charged concept: that of hierarchy. The neo-Platonic universe, in both its upper and lower chambers, was structured strictly hierarchically. Deities were distinguished in it according to their ranks in specially-designated places – *henads*. The lower hierarchical structures mirrored the upper structures. Hierarchy, for the neo-Platonists, became a superstructure that engulfed any other structure and being. So it became for the Christian theologians. One of them, who hid under the pseudonym of Dionysius Areopagite, also structured the Christian heavens and *ekklesia* hierarchically. He only substituted pagan deities with angels and linked ecclesiastical hierarchies to the divine ones.

Pseudo-Dionysius was probably one of the most a-political theologians in Christianity. Yet, unwillingly, he became one of the greatest, if not the greatest, Christian political theologian, whose thought has influenced Christian political philosophy immensely. His concept of hierarchy even now continues to be dominant in both ecclesial and political structures. It reached its heyday in the Middle Ages, when political, social and ecclesial structures became rigidly hierarchical. This hierarchy was interpreted in ontological categories, which then came to be recognised as having been established by *ius divinum*.

4 Western Copies of the Eastern Political Theologies

In the context of medieval political theology, let us return to interwar Germany, and focus on the medievalist Ernst Kantorowicz. He can be listed together with Schmitt and Peterson as a scholar who succeeded in deciphering classical theology, and extracting from it some fascinating political theories. Kantorowicz was similar to Schmitt and Peterson in many regards. He wrote in the same period and in the same place, that is to say, in interwar Germany. All three scholars had similar conservative political preferences. Kantorowicz was a German nationalist, who won an Iron Cross at Verdun, dreamed of destroying France and participated in the anti-Polish riots in his native Poznań. When the Nazis came to power, Kantorowicz expressed sympathy with some of their causes. Norman Cantor even believes that "except for the misfortune of being a Jew", Kantorowicz "was the ideal Nazi scholar and intellectual".[24] Indeed, Kantorowicz was a Jew and did not want to "deny his blood".[25] Eventually, despite his unrepented German nationalism and concurrence with many Nazi ideas, he had to leave his country and emigrated to the United States.

There, he published his masterpiece, *The King's Two Bodies*, which became an instant classic. Although it was published as early as 1957, Princeton University Press continues to reprint it to this day.[26] Kantorowicz did with the Middle Ages what Peterson did with Late Antiquity: he discovered a technology of extracting political ideas from theological formulas. In other words, both scholars discovered political theologies, which were expressed in theological terms and contributed to the legitimacy of political rulers. Both realised that at the core of those political theologies there was a Christology. For Peterson, the 'Arian' standpoint, that the Son is inferior to the Father, implied a model for the absolutist monarchy of the Christian Roman emperors. Kantorowicz dealt with the dynasties that claimed to be successors of the Roman emperors. He argued that their legitimacy rested on the Christological constructs developed by their contemporary court theologians.

Kantorowicz chose to analyse a collection of texts composed around AD 1100 by an unknown Norman theologian, who developed argumentation in favour of the exclusive prerogatives of Christian kings during the Investiture controversy. The Norman Anonymous – as he has become known in scholarship – argued that the royal office reflects the power of God: "Potestas enim regis potestas Dei est".[27] A king, as an individual person and a holder of the office, is similar to Christ in both his humanity and divinity. This was a bolder comparison than the Byzantine political theologians would permit themselves, with all their love for their rulers.

The Byzantine political theologians had developed highly sophisticated and dizzyingly nuanced theories about the imperial authority and its relationship to

---

[24] N.F. Cantor, *Inventing the Middle Ages: The Lives, Works, and Ideas of the Great Medievalists of the Twentieth Century* (New York: W. Morrow, 1991), 95.
[25] So he wrote in the letter to his mentor poet Stefan George, cited in R.E. Lerner, *Ernst Kantorowicz: A Life* (Princeton, NJ: Princeton University Press, 2018), 163.
[26] The latest reprint was made in 2016: E.H. Kantorowicz, *The King's Two Bodies: A Study in Medieval Political Theology* (Princeton, NJ: Princeton University Press, 2016).
[27] The full quote reads: "Verum si sacerdos per regem instituitur, non per potestatem hominis instituitur, sed per potestatem Dei. Potestas enim regis potestas Dei est, Dei quidem est per naturam, regis per gratiam. Unde et rex Deus et Christus est, sed per gratiam, et quicquid facit non homo simpliciter, sed Deus factus et Christus per gratiam facit. Immo ipse, qui natura Deus est et Christus, per vicarium suum hoc facit, per quem vices suas exsequitur"; *Libelli de lite imperatorum et pontificum saeculis XI. et XII. conscripti* (vol. 3 of *Monumenta Germaniae historica inde ab anno Christi quingentesimo usque ad annum millesimum et quingentesimum: Scriptores*, Hannover: Impensis Bibliopolii Hahniani, 1897), 667.35–40.

the divine. Gilbert Dagron published an encyclopedic study on this matter.[28] If we compare the theological hermeneutics of the Byzantine and Norman kingships, we see how great a theological and cultural gap there was between them. The latter seems to be a vulgar copy of the former. Even Kantorowicz, who was not a theologian and did not know the nuances of high Byzantine Christology, recognised that the theology of Norman Anonymous was deficient, with "a Nestorian and Adoptionist flavour".[29]

The Christology that the medieval Norman theologian promoted was rather poor. In particular, it was articulated in a language with theological vulgarisms, such as *persona mixta* (mixed), and forbidden words, such as *gemina* (twinned). This language was applied to the medieval kings as reflecting two natures of Christ. The word *mixture*, σύγκρασις, was taken with a large grain of suspicion in Eastern Christology – especially after it became a keyword in the Monophysite Christology of Eutyches. As for the word *twinned*, it was unheard of and indeed unthinkable in the Eastern Christological discourses. The idea of mixed or twinned person was not even Nestorian, as Kantorowicz suggested, because Nestorianism affirmed a single person (*persona*, πρόσωπον) in Christ. The Christology of the Norman Anonymous went further than Nestorianism would have gone, in dividing the *persona* of the king. Paradoxically, this political Christology appears to be quite Eutychean, which is the opposite of Nestorianism. The Byzantine monastic Eutyches taught that the humanity of Christ changed and appropriated many natural properties of divinity. This teaching is usually called Monophysitism and should be differentiated from the Miaphysite teaching of Dioscorus of Alexandria and Severus of Antioch. Although they also claimed that Christ had one nature, in their interpretation, Christ's humanity remained unchangeable and consubstantial with our humanity.

Eutycheanism insinuated an ontological alienation of Christ's humanity: the ontological status of his humanity became significantly higher than the ontological status of humankind. The anonymous Norman author in a similar manner implied that the king's power is not functional, but ontological. It has its own substance. The royal power was ontologised even more in the political theology of the Tudors in England, as Ernst Kantorowicz demonstrated in the same book, *The King's Two Bodies*. The title of this seminal study highlights its main idea, that kings were believed to have two bodies: physical and corporate. The former, the physical, was

---

28 G. Dagron, *Empereur et prêtre: étude sur le «césaropapisme» byzantin* (Paris: Gallimard, 1995); English translation: *Emperor and Priest: The Imperial Office in Byzantium* (Cambridge: Cambridge University Press, 2003).
29 Kantorowicz, *The King's Two Bodies*, 52.

mortal, while the latter, the corporate, never died. All the subjects of the English Crown were included in it. As a Tudor lawyer explained,

> The King has two Capacities, for he has two Bodies, the one whereof is a Body natural, consisting of natural Members as every other Man has, and in this he is subject to Passions and Death as other Men are; other is a Body politic, and the Members thereof are his Subjects, and he and his Subjects together compose the Corporation.[30]

The ontologisation of power, either in the form of the "twinned person" of the king, or his "corporate body", was an extreme form of political theology. Indeed, I believe, it was a heretical political theology. Once one starts making political power a thing, and not a function, it opens doors to dictatorships, wars, and other abuses. Byzantium – a prototype for many patterns of Western political theologies, which usually were copied with inaccuracies and without preserving subtleties, – did not go as far as that. True, there were other, more sophisticated and less heretical forms of ontoligisation of power in the Christian East. One of them was the already-mentioned concept of hierarchy. However, in the hierarchical structures, the power of its holder is defined not by the holder's ontological status, but by his/her place in the hierarchy. In other words, not the king *per se*, but his place had ontological gravity. That is why the dethronement of the Byzantine basileuses was a rather well-known routine,[31] and not an existential tragedy, which was so well described by Shakespeare in his *Richard II*.

5 Eastern Symphonies

Ernst Kantorowicz described Christological ideas, which underpinned the patterns of political power during the Middle Ages and early Modernity. The Christian East applied Christological models to its political patterns much earlier, in Christian Antiquity. While the West focused more on the personal power of kings, the East applied Christology to the entire complex of church-state relations. I would identify

---

[30] Justice Southcote in the case *Willion v. Berkley*, in ibid., 13.
[31] A Chinese traveller to Byzantium in the seventh century made an interesting observation about how easily the Byzantines eliminated their rulers: "Their kings are not men who last. They choose the most capable and they put him on the throne; but if a misfortune or something out of the ordinary happens in the Empire, or if the wind or the rain arrive at the wrong season, then they at once depose the emperor and put another in his place"; *Xin T'ang shu* [New book of Tang] (Beijing: Zhonghua, 1975), ch. 198, 5313–5314, cited in F. Hirth, *China and the Roman Orient: Researches Into Their Ancient and Medieval Relations as Represented in Old Chinese Records* (Chicago: Ares, 1975), 52.

three such Christological models, which had political underpinnings: Chalcedonian or Dyophysite, Miaphysite, Monothelite, and finally Nestorian. Let me give a brief characterisation of each of these Christologies.

Both Dyophysite and Miaphysite Christologies believe that humanity and divinity in Christ do not constitute distinct subjects, but have been united intrinsically into one being. On the one hand, humanity and divinity are whole, and were never alienated from what they originally had been. On the other hand, they remain distinct from one another, and have never been separated. The difference between the two approaches is that the Dyophysite Christology calls humanity and divinity "natures", and therefore speaks of two natures in Christ, while the Miaphysite Christology speaks of one nature in Christ, in order to stress the unity of Christ even more than the Dyophysite Christology does. The Monothelite Christology tried to reconcile the two above-mentioned Christologies by combining the theological language of two natures with the idea of single activity and will in Christ. Finally, the Nestorian Christology envisaged a significantly wider gap between humanity and divinity, to the extent of admitting two subjects in Christ: God and a man.

As mentioned earlier, the Byzantine ideal of church-state relations was symphonic. The classical definition of this ideal can be found in the preamble to the sixth novella promulgated by the Emperor Justinian:

> The greatest gifts that God, in his celestial benevolence, has bestowed on mankind are priesthood and sovereignty, the one serving on matters divine, and the other ruling over human affairs, and caring for them. Each proceeds from one and the same authority, and regulates human life. Thus nothing could have as great a claim on the attention of sovereigns as the honour of priests, seeing that they are the very ones who constantly offer prayer to God on the sovereigns' behalf. Hence, should the one be above reproach in every respect, and enjoy access to God, while the other keeps in correct and proper order the realm that has been entrusted to it, there will be a satisfactory harmony, conferring every conceivable benefit on the human race.[32]

"Harmony" here translates the Greek συμφωνία and Latin *consonantia*. In this model, "priesthood" and "sovereignty" are presented as two distinct political entities, which, nevertheless, come from the same source ("each proceeds from one and the same authority") and focus on the same subject: "human life". In other words, the structure of the formula of symphony is the following: unity → duality → unity.

---

32 *Corpus iuris civilis*, ed. T. Mommsen/P. Krüger/R. Schöll/W. Kroll (3 vol.; Berlin: Weidmann, 1889–1895), cited in P. Sarris (ed.), *The Novels of Justinian: A Complete Annotated English Translation*, trans. D.J.D. Miller (Cambridge: Cambridge University Press, 2018), 97–98.

Exactly the same is the structure of the Christological formula as adopted by the Council of Chalcedon in 451: unity of Christ → duality of his natures → unity of Christ.

In other words, there is an apparent coherence between how the Byzantines saw the relationship between the two natures of Christ and how they saw relations between their church and state. Justinian's symphony can hence be characterised as Chalcedonian, which is no surprise, given the support that Justinian extended to the Chalcedonian faction in the Byzantine Church.

Justinian's ideal of symphony remained an ideal. In practice, the Miaphysite formula of power was implemented. In this formula, the church and state could hardly distinguish their respective spheres of existence; even their perceptions of themselves conflated into a single theopolitical self-awareness. This can be observed, for example, in the fact that during the Byzantine period, theologians virtually never reflected on the church as an entity different from the state. Those who did reflect on it, such as John Chrysostom, usually had a non-conformist tilt in their views on church-state relations. Thus the Byzantine church and state effectively conflated into a single theopolitical nature. In this nature, they could be distinguished "only theoretically" (τῇ θεωρίᾳ μόνῃ), to use the wording of Cyril of Alexandria.[33] Paradoxically, the imperial ideologists, who were mostly Dyophysites, preferred the Miaphysite modality of church-state relations.

There was a period in Byzantine history, during the seventh century, when Christological theory and political practices converged. The emperor of the time, Heraclius (reigned 610–641), a gifted politician with an ambition of becoming a second Justinian, embarked on a project of reconciliation between the pro- and anti-Chalcedonian churches. With the assistance of his court theologians, he designed a theological formula that he believed would satisfy both quarrelling sides. On the one hand, this formula stated that Christ had one hypostasis and two natures, and this was to please the Chalcedonian side. On the other hand, the single Christ had one activity (ἐνέργεια), and this was to accommodate the anti-Chalcedonians. Later, the single activity in this formula was replaced by a single will (θέλημα). The formula was called Monoënergist/Monothelite.

This eclectic Christological formula was designed to bridge the theological and political gap between two large groups: those who supported and those who opposed the Council of Chalcedon. It can also be interpreted as having the following political implication. On the one hand, it respected the distinctiveness of the church vis-à-vis the state. On the other hand, their unity, according to this formula, had the same source of activity and one will, and that was the emperor. The Monothelite

---

[33] *Quod unus sit Christus* (CPG 5228), 736.27.

formula, which was adopted mainly for political reasons, perfectly described the church-state relations in the Eastern Roman Empire in the period, when it was passing from Antiquity to the Middle Ages. It is true that Monoënergism and Monothelitism were condemned at the ecumenical council in Constantinople in 680–681. Nevertheless, as a political formula, Monothelitism continued to define church-state relations in Byzantium until its demise.

The Monothelite political model culminated during iconoclasm. Scholars still argue about both the theological and political causes that triggered the controversy about sacred images. They agree, however, that its single promoter was the state, which forced the church to comply with its policies regarding icons. One of the main reasons that might have motivated the imperial authority was to enhance the legitimacy of this authority. Iconoclasm was an ideal case of the Monothelite symphony, when the emperor unilaterally imposed his will upon both the state and the church. It was also a case of political theology in the Schmittean sense, when theology smoothly translates into politics.

While in the Eastern Roman Empire, also known as Byzantium, there was no separation between the church and state whatsoever, with the degree of distinction between them varying from insignificant to zero, outside this empire, in the majority of cases, the church was forced into separation from the state. This produced a new model of church-state relations, which can be called Nestorian. Nestorianism, as mentioned earlier, presupposed a significant distance between divinity and humanity in Christ. This distance was caused by the interpretation of divinity and humanity as self-standing subjects: as God and a man. This interpretation was promoted by the Archbishop of Constantinople Nestorius, for which reason this Christological doctrine received his name. It was condemned at the ecumenical council in Ephesus in 431.

In a way similar to that in which the Nestorians perceived the gap between divinity and humanity in Christ, the churches outside the Roman Empire were forced to keep a distance from the state. The states that enforced such a distance were not Christian. One of the earliest examples of this, after Constantine, occurred in the Persian Empire, the eternal rival of the Greco-Roman world. The Persians, with several exceptions, tolerated Christianity, but did not offer Christian bishops any symphonic favour – even though the latter tried hard to attain it. The Christian community in Persia had to live in a fairly pluralistic society with no preferences awarded from the state. Occasionally it was persecuted. The majority in this minority consisted of the Nestorians, mainly Christians from Eastern Syria, who refused to comply with the council of Ephesus and thus were expelled from Roman soil.

This experience of living in a pluralistic society, with no benefits from the state, was painful at first for the church but soon proved to be to its advantage. The Nestorian Christians, also known as Assyrians, made good use of their experiences of survival in the Persian environment, namely, in their mission to Asia. These experiences allowed them to establish themselves successfully in the countries and societies as impenetrable to foreign influence as that of the Chinese. I believe the success of this mission is connected to the Nestorian model of relationship with the states where this church sent its missionaries.

At the time when the Chalcedonian churches in Byzantium lived through Miaphysite sorts of symphony, the Miaphysite churches, which after the Arab conquest of Syria and Egypt found themselves under the control of the Caliphate, had to embark on the Nestorian model of relations with the Muslim state, – even though they despised everything Nestorian. In effect, most of those churches, which we know as Oriental, continue to live according to the same Nestorian pattern. Most Byzantine churches had to adopt the same pattern, when the Ottomans established their own state on the ruins of Byzantium. The Nestorian model of church-state relations, which the Eastern churches have experienced since at least the fifth century, was not dissimilar to the Jeffersonian "wall" and other modern models of separation between the church and state. Thus the Eastern churches pioneered the models of both unity and separation from the state, and the Western churches followed them.

I mentioned above that the churches in the East were forced into the Nestorian model of relations with the state. This model was never their choice. They always preferred the one nature model whenever it was possible, or even when it was impossible. Modernity, with its 'disestablishmentness', caused a lot of pain to both Western and Eastern churches, – probably more than with its secularisation and 'modernism'. The Catholic Church suffered 'phantom pains' after being stripped of much of its own political power, while the 'phantom pains' for many Eastern churches came from losing privileged relationships with the state. Following their symphonic instinct and suffering from the deprivation of political influence, the churches usually did not miss the slightest opportunity to collaborate with political regimes, even when these regimes were hostile.

Perhaps the most bizarre kind of symphony that ever occurred in the history of Christianity was the one with the regime whose established religion was militant atheism. I would characterise the *modus vivendi* of the Russian Orthodox Church in the Soviet Union as symphonic. The formula of this symphony was articulated by Metropolitan Sergiy Stragorodsky, later the Patriarch of Moscow, and published by the central Communist newspaper *Izvestia* in 1927: "We want to be Orthodox and at the same time do recognise the Soviet Union as our civic homeland, the joys and successes of which are our joys and successes, and whose failures are our failures".[34] Needless to say that among the greatest joys of the Soviet homeland would be to eliminate any religion altogether.

---

[34] First published in the Soviet newspaper *Izvestia*, 18 August 1927.

Many historians argue, and this is also an official line of the Moscow Patriarchate, that the church had two bad choices: to be exterminated or to collaborate with the regime, with a hope of survival. Therefore, the best option that the church had, even though it was not a good option, was to collaborate with the Communist regime. Others counter-argue that the church by all means had to avoid collaboration with the atheistic regime. As an alternative, the Christians could go underground and, if needed, had to die as martyrs. In effect, many underground groups, all of which of dubious canonical status, mushroomed during the waves of the Soviet persecutions. Collaboration with the state at any price did not save the official church from persecutions. Most of its bishops, priests and monastics were killed or exiled to the Gulags, and most churches were shut down or destroyed.

Those Russian hierarchs who survived Stalin's purges in the 1930s, were recruited by the Soviet government after the Second World War to propagate in the world the advantages of the Communist ideology. A new kind of symphony was established. Its scope, however, was very narrow: this symphony served only the purposes of Soviet propaganda abroad, and it benefited only a minuscule group of hierarchs. The majority of ordinary faithful continued to suffer and were restricted in their basic rights. Again, some people would argue today that the church did not have any other choice but to cooperate with the state. However, I believe there was something more to this cooperation than simply choosing between two bad options. It was a desperate, and sometimes subconscious, need to have a political partner, even if this partner wanted to kill you. Some would call it the Stockholm syndrome. I would call it symphonic syndrome.

6 Orthodoxy and Totalitarian Ideologies

The same symphonic syndrome moved the Orthodox churches to support radical nationalist regimes and ideologies, which mushroomed in the traditionally Orthodox countries in the interwar period. In addition to the custom of treating *any* political regime as a partner, the churches were motivated by what we now call traditional values, which were usually promoted by fascist and nationalist regimes and ideologies. Most Orthodox countries in different periods of the twentieth century lived through conservative dictatorships or ideologies close to fascism. They were in most cases modelled on Italian Fascism,[35] and sometimes came close to Nazism.

---

35 See D.G. Williamson, *The Age of the Dictators: A Study of the European Dictatorships, 1918–53* (Harlow, UK: Routledge, 2007), 132.

The Italian word *clericofascista*, coined by Fr Luigi Sturzo in the 1920s,[36] is also applicable to many clergy, hierarchs, primates and even saints in the Orthodox churches during the last century.

One of the most obvious examples is the Romanian National Legionary State, which existed in 1940–1941. It featured a one-party regime with a strong agenda of Orthodox conservatism. This state was controlled by the right-wing nationalist Legion of Archangel Michael (Legiunea Arhanghelului Mihail). This was a clerical movement and then a party, with about 30% of its members in the parliament after the elections in 1937 being priests. A priest from this movement wrote in its heyday: "A true priest will therefore be a Legionnaire by the nature of things, just as a Legionnaire will be in his turn, and again by the nature of things, a Legionnaire, the best son of the Church".[37] Most scholars agree that the Legion was a movement with a strong fascist tilt.

There were less numerous movements in other Orthodox countries, which had a similar bent. One of them, Assembly (Zbor), was organised in Serbia by Dimitrije Ljotić. While not as popular as the Romanian Legion, the Serbian Zbor had many similarities with the former: both combined a conservative and nationalistic political agenda with a strong religious motivation. Zbor was also supported by influential hierarchs, one of them being bishop Nikolaj Velimirović. Scholars still argue which kind of fascism Ljotić's ideology was close to.[38] One can easily recognise in it some classical fascist features, such as the idea of a corporatist state, – similar to Benito Mussolini's "lo stato corporativo".[39] Unlike Mussolini, however, Ljotić regarded religion as the core of national identity.

Most Orthodox thinkers and hierarchs outspoken in promoting ultra-conservative and ultra-nationalist agendas in the interwar period felt closer to Italian Fascism than to German Nazism. Nevertheless, from time to time they uttered some words of approval of Hitler, too. The above-mentioned Nikolaj Velimirović, for instance, in his article "The Nationalism of St Sava", published in 1935, urged his readers to "render homage to the present German leader, who [...] realised that

---

36 Sturzo coined the word in the interview with *La Stampa* (10 February 1924) and then used it in later publications, such as L. Sturzo, *Popolarismo e fascismo* (Torino: Gobetti, 1924), and L. Sturzo, "La politica dei clerico-fascisti", in L. Sturzo, *Pensiero antifascista* (Torino: Gobetti, 1925), 7–16.
37 I. Imbrescu, *Biserica și mișcarea legionară* (Bucharest: Cartea Romaneasca, 1940), 201, cited in R. Griffin/M. Feldman, *The "Fascist Epoch"* (vol. 4 of *Fascism: Critical Concepts in Political Science*, London: Routledge, 2004), 132.
38 See M. Falina, "Between 'Clerical Fascism' and Political Orthodoxy: Orthodox Christianity and Nationalism in Interwar Serbia", in M. Feldman/M. Turda/T. Georgescu (ed.), *Clerical Fascism in Interwar Europe* (London: Routledge, 2014), 35–46, on p. 33.
39 See B. Mussolini, *Lo stato corporativo* (Firenze: Vallecchi, 1938).

nationalism without religion is an anomaly, a cold and insecure mechanism".[40] Another prominent conservative hierarch of that time, the Primate of the Russian Orthodox Church Outside Russia, Metropolitan Anastasiy Gribanovskiy, praised Hitler in 1938 with the following words:

> Not only the German nation commemorates you with fervent love and devotion to the Throne of the Highest: the best people of all nations, who wish you peace and justice, see you as a leader in the world struggle for peace and truth. [...] Your feat for the German people and the greatness of the German Empire made you an exemplary model worthy of imitation, and a model of how one should love one's people and one's country, how one should stand for national treasures and eternal values. [...] May God strengthen you and the German people in the fight against hostile forces, who wish death of our people. May He give you, your country, your Government and the army good health, prosperity and all the good haste for many years.[41]

Both Fascism and Nazism were quite popular in the conservative circles of the Russian White immigration to the West. Some immigrants collaborated with these regimes, and some even provided inspiration for them. This inspiration came from a particular direction of what we can call Russian political theology, as it developed at the beginning of the twentieth century.

Political theology was not a part of the official theological curriculum in the Romanovs' Russia. It emerged outside this curriculum, and immediately took two opposite directions. One direction was liberal and accommodating for the developments in the progressive part of Russian society. That part wanted emancipation from monarchy, constitution, equal rights for all strata of society, and so on. A political theology that reflected these desiderata was articulated by such prominent figures in Russian religious philosophy as Vladimir Solovyov, Sergei Bulgakov and Nikolai Berdyaev. It influenced the programme of *aggiornamento* adopted by the council of the Russian Church in 1917–1918. I believe this council was a forerunner of the Second Vatican Council.

The other direction of the Russian political theology at that time was reactionary and populist. It tried theologically to substantiate monarchy, was anti-modernist and anti-democratic. Among the protagonists in this direction of political theology were some prominent hierarchs, including Metropolitan Antoniy Khrapovitskiy,

---

40 N. Velimirović, *Nacionalizam Svetog Save: Predavanje održano na proslavi nedelje pravoslavlja u Beogradu 1935* [The Nationalism of Saint Sava: Lecture Held at the Celebration of the Sunday of Orthodoxy in Belgrade in 1935], (Belgrade: Udruženje srpskog pravoslavnog sveštenstva Arhiepiskopije beogradsko-karlovačke, 1935), 21; English translation in M. Falina, "Between 'Clerical Fascism' and Political Orthodoxy: Orthodox Christianity and Nationalism in Interwar Serbia," *Totalitarian Movements & Political Religions* 8/2 (2007): 247–258, on p. 253.
41 Gribanovskiy's message published in *Tserkovnaya Zhizn* 5/6 (1938), 96.

who later founded the conservative Russian Orthodox Church Outside Russia, mentioned above in connection to greetings to Hitler, and Archbishop Serafim Sobolev. The latter, for instance, believed that democracy is a diabolic political system. He wrote a book entitled *Russian Ideology*, which can be considered a manifesto of Russian conservative political theology. Recently, the Moscow Patriarchate proclaimed him a saint.[42]

7 Anti-Semitism

I should now like to focus my microscope on a figure who contributed to this same conservative political theology in a special way. His name is Sergei Nilus, and he composed pietistic pamphlets and books for the people. His approach to political theology was *völkisch*. He picked up stories and prophecies from the past and extracted from them lessons about the divine character of monarchy, and how gravely those who challenge this institution sin. He became famous for popularising the figure of Seraphim of Sarov, a Russian monk who flourished in the first three decades of the nineteenth century. Nilus published spiritual conversations of this monk with one Nikolay Motovilov, and concluded from these conversations how important it is for his contemporaries to support the Romanov dynasty wholeheartedly.

Recent studies have established that those conversations were to a great extent fictional.[43] Even more fictional was an appendix attached to their publication. This appendix is known as the *Protocols of the Elders of Zion*,[44] and they were published for the first time by Nilus. Scholars still argue by whom and where this forgery was produced. Very likely, the imperial Russian intelligence agencies were behind the *Protocols*. The purpose of this appendix was to compromise the Jewish participants in the anti-tsarist movement, and this purpose cohered with the general goal of the book: to bring convincing arguments in favour of the monarchy and to defy its enemies.

The *Protocols* became wildly popular reading in pre-revolutionary Russia. Even Tsar Nicholas II Romanov read them with a pencil in his hand. After the Bolshevik revolution, they were transmitted to the West. It is believed that the person

---

42 S. Sobolev, *Russkaya ideologiya* [Russian ideology], (Sofia, s.n., 1939).
43 See V. Stepashkin, *Seraphim Sarovskij* [Seraphim of Sarov], (Moscow: Molodaya gvardiya, 2018).
44 S. Nilus, *Velikoe v malom i antikhrist kak blizkaya politicheskaya vozmozhnost, Zapiski pravoslavnogo* [The big within the small and the Antichrist as a imminent political possibility, notes of an Orthodox], (Tsarkoe Selo: Tipografiya Tsarskoeselskogo komiteta Krasnogo kresta, 1905).

who brought the *Protocols* to Germany was Pyotr Shabelsky-Bork, a devoted royalist and participant in the anti-Bolshevik military campaign. After this campaign failed, he was rescued by the Germans during the winter of 1918–1919.[45] When in Berlin, Shabelsky-Bork met a German nationalist, Ludwig Müller von Hausen. Von Hausen helped publish the first German translation of the *Protocols* in 1920 in the newspaper *Völkischer Beobachter*. The *Protocols* became a best-seller in Germany and, no doubt, contributed to the rapid spread of Nazi anti-Semitic propaganda.

The *Protocols* also inspired many Orthodox in other countries. For instance, in 1926 a Serbian devotional group, Bohomoljci, led by the above-mentioned bishop Nikolaj Velimirović, disseminated the *Protocols* in Serbia.[46] Anti-Semitism, inspired by the *Protocols*, continues to be a part of the modern Schmittean versions of Orthodox political theology, even today. Soon after liberation from Soviet atheism, the largest Russian monastery, the Lavra of St Sergiy, along with urgently needed spiritual literature, published a collection, *Russia Before the Second Coming*.[47] It was a compilation of quotes and 'prophecies', often falsified, about the 'powers of evil' working against Russia. The West and Jews were named among those powers, and the *Protocols of the Elders of Zion* were included in the edition.

8 Nationalism

Bishop Nikolaj Velimirović, and with him many other conservative Orthodox political theologians, counterposed Orthodox nationalism to the secular West. He accused the West of anthropocentrism,[48] which has substituted God with man. The irony, however, is that nationalism is a Western secular construct. In the capacity of an ideology, it emerged as an organic part of the Enlightenment project. Adaman-

---

45 Michael Kellogg found this information in a gestapo report from April 1935. See M. Kellogg, *The Russian Roots of Nazism: White Émigrés and the Making of National Socialism, 1917–1945* (Cambridge: Cambridge University Press, 2008), 63.
46 See A.V. Prusin, *Serbia Under the Swastika: A World War II Occupation* (Urbana, IL: University of Illinois Press, 2017), 127.
47 S. Fomin, *Rossiya pered vtornym prishestviem* [Russia before the second coming], (Moscow: Svyato-Troitskaya Sergieva Lavra, 1993). In the period 1993–2005, around two hundred thousand copies of the book were sold; see V. Shnirelman, "Eskhatologiya, prorochestva o konze sveta i antisemitizm v postsovetskoj Rossii" [Eschatology, prophecies about the end of the world and anti-Semitism in post-soviet Russia], *Forum novejshej vostochnoevropejskoj istorii i kultury* 1 (2015), 306.
48 See R. Bigović, *Od svečoveka do Bogočoveka: hrišćanska filosofija vladike Nikolaja Velimirovića* [From the Holy man to the God-man: the Christian philosophy of Bishop Nikolaj Velimirović] (Belgrade: Raška Škola, 1998), 363.

tios Koraïs, who was among the main proponents of nationalism on Orthodox soil, discussed it first in the Parisian Société des observateurs de l'homme – a quintessentially anthropocentric society.

After having been imported to the Orthodox countries, nationalism combined with the religious identity of the peoples there. Its secularist pedigree was thoroughly camouflaged. An ancient and specifically Eastern structure of the Orthodox Church, autocephaly, facilitated the appropriation of nationalist ideologies in the Orthodox world. In the West, nationalism clashed with the universalist structure of the Catholic Church, which responded by condemning it in the forms of Gallicanism or Febronianism. In the East, nationalism cohered with the autocephalous (meaning self-headed, independent) structure of the local Orthodox Churches. Because of the compatibility between the autocephalous structure of Orthodoxy and ethnic states, nationalism – originally a secular ideology – was readily adopted in the Orthodox Church. It became a quasi-religious phenomenon, without clashing very much with religion proper and sometimes even substituting the latter. As a result, there are more people who identify themselves as Orthodox than those who believe in God.[49]

Raymond Aron's term *religion séculière* describes Orthodox nationalism best. A particular instance of this *religion séculière* is an ideologeme that emerged recently, that of the Russian world. It is not exactly the same as the nationalistic ideologies in most Southern or Eastern European countries, which are usually identified with one nation. The nationalism of the Russian world is supra-ethnic and indeed neo-imperial. It exploits culture, language, and faith to rebuild the Russian world within the framework of the Romanovs' Russia and, if possible, Stalin's Soviet Union. This ideology has inspired the two wars that were waged on the European continent during the twenty-first century: the one on the territory of Georgia in 2008, and the other on the territory of Ukraine. The ideology of the Russian world sometimes presents itself as political Orthodoxy. In effect, both are similar to that particular case of political theology which was promoted by Carl Schmitt and opposed by Erik Peterson.

---

[49] See Pew Research Center, "Religious Belief and National Belonging in Central and Eastern Europe" (10 May 2017), https://assets.pewresearch.org/wp-content/uploads/sites/11/2017/05/15120244/CEUP-FULL-REPORT.pdf (accessed 12 January 2021).

9 Conclusions

Politicised religion, in conclusion, is still very active in our days and causes a great deal of evil. However, it is probably as ancient as religion itself. In the period of Antiquity, politicised religion was a norm – the only form of religion that people publicly practised. Christ brought a change, when he said, disappointingly for many of his followers: "My kingdom is not of this world" (John 18:36). Early Christianity followed this non-conformist principle, which was quite a departure from the common practices of Antiquity. The hostility of the Roman Empire to the Christian communities corroborated the Christian non-conformist attitude. When the hostile tide started changing to a more favourable one, Christianity faced the challenge of getting back on the track of the old Greco-Roman religions: to become public, serve *salus populi romani*, provide legitimacy for the political authorities, and so on. A significant part of the church followed that track, but not all of it. A number of non-conformist movements emerged that endeavoured to preserve the early Christian ethos. The most significant among them became known as monasticism.

The Christian East has authored most models of politicised religion. The West often followed the East, with a little original input. The Western copies of politicised religion usually were not as refined as the Eastern originals. These original models were embodied in the Eastern Roman Empire, known to us now as Byzantium, in Late Antiquity, and in the Western Christendom of the Middle Ages.

Modernity, with its Hobbesean and Jeffersonian separation between church and state, challenged the old symphony-based models of politicised religion. This religion, nevertheless, has survived even the unfavourable conditions of modernity. It was reinvented and recast in many new forms. This time, the West led, and the East followed. They often took their inspiration from the Romanticised Middle Ages and Romanticised Byzantium. Some countries in the West, and later in the East, being tired of modernisation of their societies, tried to resurrect the glories of *Germania* or of τὸ Βυζάντιον. Some even now try to recreate the Romanticised and ideal version of the medieval Holy Rus. The results are always the same: on the basis of Romantic blueprints they usually end up with totalitarian regimes.

These regimes utilise what Erik Peterson criticised as political theology. We should probably not follow Peterson in condemning political theology wholesale. After all, this term was rehabilitated after the Second World War within the framework of the so-called theology after Auschwitz. Its founding father, Jürgen Moltmann was, by the way, influenced by Erik Peterson.[50] Since then, it has become one of the most studied theological disciplines in the world. Modern political theol-

---

50 See R. Williams, *Arius: Heresy and Tradition* (London: SCM Press, 2001), 14.

ogy studies all forms of interaction between the church and public square, a very respectable and legitimate field. What Peterson criticised could be called not political theology, but by more appropriate names: secular or political religion. It can also be called, and sometimes it calls itself, political Orthodoxy, political Catholicism, political Protestantism, and so on.

This phenomenon may have many names, but its quintessence is the same. It was articulated by Hannah Arendt, a secular Jewish philosopher who understood some things about Christianity better than many Christian theologians did in her time: "If we try to inspire public-political life once more with 'religious passion' or to use religion as a means of political distinctions, the result may very well be the transformation and perversion of religion into an ideology".[51]

She apparently meant the totalitarian ideologies of Communism, Fascism, and Nazism. This list, however, can be expanded and should include the ideologies that seem to have been appropriated by Christianity, to the point of merging the latter with the former. Such is, for instance, nationalism, which is particularly strong in the world of Eastern Christianity. The most recent ideology of the Russian world can also be added to the list. These ideologies demonstrate that politicised religion leads to substituting theology with ideology as its simulacrum, the transcendent *beyond* with the visible *here*, religion with politics. It causes the alienation of religion as such and opens doors for conflicts, tragedies, and wars.

---

51 Arendt, "Religion and Politics", 384.

Susanne Schröter
Islam, Politics, and Society in Germany

This article will focus on a topic that is causing much controversy in many European countries, that is the relationship between politics, society and Islam, and will outline the situation in Germany where the debate is primarily about the question of whether certain forms of Islam are compatible with European values and human rights or whether we need a European or German Islam that is adapted to the local conditions.

Muslims in Germany are a small minority, but in the cities a rapidly growing one that is demanding political recognition. What recognition means is a matter debated among both Muslims and non-Muslims. Fundamental in this regard is the question as to how the constitutional right to freedom of religion can and ought to be interpreted and implemented. Christian symbols are increasingly disappearing from the public eye, the churches have seen a considerable decline in membership, and the enforcement of church norms has been severely restricted by court rulings in recent years. Most Germans are atheists, agnostics, or treat religion as a private matter. This is the result of an ongoing secularisation process. By contrast, many Muslims explicitly emphasise their religiosity. They want to be recognisable as Muslims through their clothing, fight for the visual representation of Islamic symbols in the public, and demand the implementation of Islamic norms, for example in schools. Other citizens with a so-called Muslim background, on the other hand, urge against a strengthening of Islamist organisations. Above all those who were persecuted in their home countries because of their opposition to Islamic norms accuse German politics of naivety.

1 The German 'Orientmania'

Muslims are the 'others' to the European present. Among the immigrant groups they occupy a special status that is justified mainly on the basis of their religion. Is this an indicator of so-called Islamophobic sentiments that go way back in the past, as is claimed by some scholars and activists?

In the German historical context Islam has by no means been associated with negative connotations alone, even though romanticised fantasies of the Orient did, to an extent, co-exist with threatening ones. A rather positive view of Islam was due

This text is an edited version of the lecture given at the EuARe 2020 conference.

Open Access. © 2023 Susanne Schröter, published by De Gruyter. This work is licensed under the Creative Commons Attribution 4.0 International License.
https://doi.org/10.1515/9783111229102-004

in large part to prominent intellectuals such as Johann Wolfgang von Goethe, who in his later years took great interest in Oriental poetry, particularly the works of the Persian poet Hafez, whom he referred to as his spiritual brother. This inspired him to write his *West-östlicher Divan*, a collection of lyrical verses and scholarly reflections, which was published in 1819 and up to this day fuels speculations that near the end of his life the German poet converted to Islam. A similar fascination with the Orient led to the collection of objects housed in the Turkish Chamber at Dresden Castle, where gifts and war booty from the Ottoman Empire are on display. Augustus II the Strong, Elector of Saxony, and later also King of Poland, was so smitten with Orient-mania that at festive events he dressed as a sultan and hosted oriental tournaments, for which he even imported camels and Arabian horses. The German fascination with the Orient and with Islam also had an impact on the history of science. As early as in 1728, Johann Christian Clodius was appointed in Leipzig to be the first professor of Arabic at a German university. He established German Oriental Studies with a focus on the study of Islam, Arabic philology, and Islamic history. Scholars such as Heinrich Leberecht Fleischer, who turned Leipzig into an internationally renowned centre of research on the Orient, and Theodor Nöldeke, who in 1860 published a history of the Qur'an and in 1863 a seminal biography of the Prophet Muhammad, were important pioneers in the establishment of the field. In 1845, German Orientalists founded the German Oriental Society with the aim of promoting the academic study of Oriental languages and cultures; this scholarly society still exists today. This was the situation with scholars and the nobility. But how about politics?

While German political expansion into the Orient was negligible compared to that of England or France, Germany did try to wield influence. For example, archaeologist Max von Oppenheim, who had previously led excavations at Tell Halaf in Syria, worked for German intelligence in Constantinople during the First World War, from where he tried to stage an uprising against the British. At the same time and as part of this mission, the German Ministry of Foreign Affairs issued a magazine with the title *al-Jihād*, in which that uprising was propagated as a holy war. In 1914, a prison camp for Muslim prisoners of the British and French armies was erected, together with a mosque, in Wünstorf near Berlin. Since then, Muslim civic associations have existed in Germany. One of them is the Islamic community of Berlin, on whose initiative the first permanent mosque was established in 1924 in the Berlin district of Wilmersdorf. During the Second World War, the National Socialist Party entered into a rather unholy alliance with the Grand Mufti of Jerusalem, which was based largely on their shared anti-Semitism, and the Wilmersdorf mosque was instrumentalised for war-time propaganda events. A close cooperation between Islamists and National Socialists was established, in which Muhammad Amin al-Husayni, the Mufti of Jerusalem, became a German ally. He shared Heinrich Himmler's idea of the complete annihilation of all Jews, fled to Germany after an Arab uprising had been defeated, and helped build a Muslim SS division in Bosnia and Herzegovina. The recruitment of Muslims for the Wehrmacht and SS was organised and planned, and from 1940 Muslims fought against the Soviet Union in German uniforms and under German command.

2 Islam in the Immigration Society

Ordinary Germans neither read Persian poetry, nor did they participate in intelligence operations. Their knowledge of the Islamic world was scant, and what little they knew was drawn from fairy tales. Until the mid-60s of the twentieth century, Muslims living in Germany continued to represent a tiny, exotic minority. But since then this has changed significantly. In 1961, the German and Turkish governments concluded a bilateral labour recruitment agreement. In 1963, Germany entered into similar agreements with Morocco and in 1965 with Tunisia. In 1971, provisions were made to regulate and facilitate the immigration of workers and their families into Germany. As a result, hundreds of thousands of so far mostly male migrants brought their wives and children to Germany. From the mid-1970s, Germany witnessed increasing immigration from conflict areas and war zones. Subsequently, students also began to immigrate into the country. The Muslim migrants came together in cultural associations and mosque communities and lived strictly separated from the German majority society. The latter did not see any problem with this, since everyone involved agreed that the stay of both refugees and students, as well as of the 'guest workers' in Germany, would remain temporary. Today, more than fifty years after the agreements were signed, Germany sees itself as an immigration country, and the commitment to diversity and pluralism has replaced the old, homogenising, leading culture.

Nevertheless, discussions about Islam and particularly about the question of whether Islam belongs to Germany, continue to be controversial. In October 2010, in a speech delivered on the occasion of the twentieth anniversary of German unification, German Federal President (*Bundespräsident*) Christian Wulff stated that, like Christianity or Judaism, Islam had become an integral part of Germany. A few months later, in early March 2011, the newly appointed German Minister of the Interior, Hans-Peter Friedrich, proclaimed the opposite: he insisted that there is, in fact, no historical evidence supporting the claim that Islam is a part of Germany. Instead, Friedrich emphasised Germany's Christian-'occidental' roots. Wulff's successor to the office of Federal President, Joachim Gauck, a former Protestant pastor, relativised the position taken by his predecessor by stating that not Islam *per se*, but rather Muslims living in Germany, belong to Germany. Ten years have passed, but the majority of the population still believes that Islam does not belong to Germany.

Some of these sceptics can be included with the right-wing camp and are primarily led by xenophobic sentiments, others only reject political Islam, and a third group is involved in interreligious dialogue, campaigning for measures to guarantee Muslims better participation in society. Politicians have made many efforts to involve Muslims in cooperation.

Officially, German Islam politics began in 2007 with the German Islam Conference, which was initiated in 2006 by Wolfgang Schäuble, then Minister of the Interior. The German Islam Conference represents the most influential forum of political dialogue with Muslim communities at the national level. Representatives of the umbrella organisations, but also critical intellectuals were invited to the first meeting. After a while, the critics of Islamism were excluded – a result of the intervention of the Islamists.

Since the first German Islam Conference, much has been undertaken. The German Council of Science and Humanities had recommended the establishment of Islamic studies centres and chairs in Islamic theology at German universities. These centres have been established at the universities of Münster/Osnabrück, Erlangen/Nuremberg, Tübingen, Frankfurt/Giessen and Berlin. Other locations will follow, as the establishment of Islamic theologies is considered a political prestige project. In 2003, the states of Lower Saxony, Bavaria, North Rhine-Westphalia, and Rhineland-Palatinate initiated pilot projects that introduced faith-based courses on Islam in schools, and the state of Baden-Wurttemberg followed suit in 2006. In 2012 such faith-based courses on Islam were offered as part of the regular curriculum for Muslim pupils at selected schools. Hesse was the first federal state to establish regular Islamic lessons. Representatives of Muslim organisations are members of broadcasting councils and integration conferences, and several federal states signed state treaties with them. However, some of these contracts have now been terminated, others are under discussion. In order to understand why this is the case, it is necessary to take a look not only at non-Muslim societies, but also at Muslims.

Who are the Muslims in Germany and who speaks for them?

If we use various specific ways of understanding Islam as an indicator, we come up with the following classification system: 1) Salafists; 2) traditionalists; 3) legal Islamists; 4) members of diverse Sufi-groups; 5) liberal or reform-oriented Muslims; 6) secular citizens with a so-called Muslim background.

3 Salafists

Let us start with the Salafists, a diverse group of Muslims who aim to revive an ideal Islamic society as they imagine it to have existed during the seventh and eighth centuries in Mecca and Medina. They seek guidance from the *Salaf*, the pious forefathers of Islam, namley the early followers of Muhammad, his companions and their descendants, who are considered to have led exemplary lives that were particularly pleasing to God. Salafi ideology is characterised by crude pairs of opposites such as Muslims versus non-Muslims, *ḥalāl* versus *ḥarām*, and simple directions for action. Salafis are convinced of the superiority of Islam over other world views, and believe that Allah will condemn all non-Muslims – called infidels (*kuffār*) – to suffering in eternal hellfire after death. Infidels include Muslims who do not share the Salafis' definition of Islam, most notably Shi'ite, Sufis, members of the Ahmadiyya, and progressive Muslims. Salafis hold that God has entrusted them with the task of converting the *kuffār*. This is the reason for their untiring missionary work (*Da'wah*), for example, the "Lies!" campaign in which Salafi men distributed free copies of the Qur'an in pedestrian zones, trying to attract new members. While boys of any age are recruited for the *Da'wah* and also for the *jihad*, women are rarely visible in public, as Salafi ideology forbids them to leave the house except for very sound reasons.

Salafists purport to emulate the first Muslims in every respect; hence, particular importance is attached to outward appearance: the ankle-length robes (*jellabah*) and beards of the men, and the strict concealment of women's bodies (*ḥijāb*) including the face veil (*niqāb*). The conspicuous garments, as well as the campaigns including prayers at busy downtown places, were good publicity and attracted public attention.

As everywhere in Europe, young German jihadists joined foreign militias, such as al-Qaida, the al-Shabab militia or the so-called Islamic State, which has now suffered a bruising military defeat. Nevertheless, the number of Salafists and jihadists in Germany remains at a high level. Salafists are particularly successful among young people and have an above-average number of converts in their ranks.

4 Traditionalists

Traditionalists make up the majority of members of mosque communities where they appreciate the traditions of their homeland being practised. Many of them do not speak the German language at all or only poorly. When they talk about homeland, they mean their country of origin, with which they have close ties and where they invest money in property. Germany has remained a foreign country for them and they strive to preserve the values of their homeland, which means above all Islamic and patriarchal values. Traditionalists practise Islam as they have learned it in their communities and as the imam teaches it in Friday sermons. Many of them are very conservative and believe that a fundamentalist understanding of Islam is correct.

They are also conservative politically. A majority of those with a Turkish background vote for the Justice and Development Party (Adalet ve Kalkınma Partisi, AKP) and see Recep Tayyip Erdoğan as their president. Traditionalists do not necessarily, but in many cases, join the organisations of political Islam.

5 Legal Islamists, or Organisations of Political Islam

There is widespread agreement among political actors in Germany that Salafism should be viewed as extremism. This is different for actors from the sphere of legalist political Islam, which also includes the Muslim Brotherhood.

Legalist political Islam in Germany is organised into four umbrella organisations.

The largest of them is the Turkish-Islamic Union of the Institute of Religion (Diyanet İşleri Türk-İslam Birliği, DİTİB). It was founded by the Turkish Ministry of Religion, Diyanet, which is directly under the control of the Turkish president. The DİTİB runs about 1,000 mosques in Germany. In terms of finances, personnel, politics and organisation, it is entirely dependent on the Diyanet. The imams of DİTİB are Turkish officials and sent by Ankara for a fixed period of time. Their salary comes from Ankara. In the past, DİTİB has repeatedly been used for spreading Turkish state propaganda, and imams were suspected of gathering intelligence for the Turkish secret services. Historical battles have been re-enacted in mosques by children so as to strengthen a Turkish-nationalist identity, and war propaganda has been spread after the Turkish military repeatedly invaded Syria. Generally, DİTİB has taken an anti-integrative course. Erdoğan is known to argue that too much integration should be seen as a violation of human rights. In 2019, he abused DİTİB in order to hold a conference in Cologne, at which the idea of a European Islam was publicly rejected. Instead, a unity of Islam under Turkish leadership was conjured up. Participants included not only DİTİB and Diyanet officials, but also representatives of the Millî Görüş movement and the Muslim Brotherhood.

The Islamic community Millî Görüş is the second major umbrella organisation. Even more than DİTİB, the Millî Görüş movement has been clearly regarded as Islamist since its inception. Its founder, Necmettin Erbakan, considered it a means to his ends: that is the transformation of Turkey into an Islamic state. In Germany it faced an even more radical split than in Turkey when the charismatic preacher Cemaleddin Kaplan and his son Metin, who were persecuted in Turkey because of anti-state activities, had obtained asylum in Germany, and began to gather followers. Metin Kaplan established relations with several jihadist groups and proclaimed a caliphate in Cologne in the 1980s.

The third large association is the Association of Islamic Cultural Centres (Verband der Islamischen Kulturzentren (VIKZ). It is a group rigidly closed to the outside world, and its members live in keeping with Islamic norms. Particularly for young people, this segregation is a problem. The VIKZ is tightly organised, managed from Turkey like DİTİB and Millî Görüş, and also represents a fundamentalist Islam. In contrast to DİTİB and Millî Görüs, it primarily acts internally and less as a political player.

The fourth umbrella organisation is called Central Council of Muslims in Germany (Zentralrat der Muslime in Deutschland, ZMD). Unlike its name suggests, it is a conglomeration of very heterogeneous subgroups. The leader and the face of the Council of Muslims is Aiman Mazyek, who presents himself as a staunch democrat in the public and likes to have his picture taken with German leaders. His deputy Mehmet Alparslan Çelebi belongs to the Turkish ultranationalists and is the son of their founder Musa Serdar Çelebi, who was in custody for two years for being involved in an attack against Pope John Paul II. The largest subgroup under the umbrella of the ZMD is the Union of Turkish-Islamic Cultural Associations in Europe (Avrupa Türk-Islam Birligi, ATIB), an ultranationalist group that formerly terrorised left-wing activists and ethnic minorities. Its members associate themselves with grey wolves – an allusion to the totem animal of a right-wing scene in Turkey. The wolf also refers to Islamist values, true to the Turkish-Islamic synthesis of Turkish nationalist Islamists.

The second subgroup is made up of organisations that belong to the global network of the Muslim Brotherhood. As I have already mentioned, political connections between Muslim Brothers and Germans go back to the time of National Socialism, when shared anti-Semitism and the will to exterminate Jews constituted a connecting link. After the Second World War, there were several waves in which Muslims migrated to Germany. The first group of Muslims consisted of former allies of the Wehrmacht or the SS. Influential former Nazis wanted to assist Muslim comrades from the Central Asian Soviet Republics to build a religious infrastructure in Germany. A mosque construction commission was founded, whose first chairman was a former SS leader from Uzbekistan who had been involved in the suppression of the Warsaw Uprising. This structure was later taken over by members of the Muslim Brotherhood, some of whom came as refugees from Egypt to Germany, others as students. These beginnings subsequently evolved into widely ramified structures that are of importance today. Noteworthy was the role of converts within the first generation of German post-war Muslims who orientated themselves to a Muslim Brotherhood ideology. One of them was Fatima Grimm, a mother of five, author of the magazine *Al-Islam* and translator of the works of Islamists such as Abul A'la Maududi and Sayyid Qutb. One of her leaflets dealt with the Islamic education of children, in which she campaigned that boys should be educated for the *jihad*.

Organisations close to the Muslim Brotherhood have founded a number of network organisations both internationally and in Germany, such as the European Council for Fatwa and Research, which theologically justify a rejection of secular norms and promote a Muslim counter-society. The Muslim Brotherhood organisations in Germany include many mosques that are close to Salafism and either perform Salafist rhetoric in Friday sermons or invite well-known Salafist preachers to preach and hold Islam seminars.

The third organisation of importance under the umbrella of the Council is the Islamic Centre Hamburg (Islamisches Zentrum Hamburg, IZH), which was founded by the Iranian regime and is responsible for exporting the ideology of the Islamic Revolution. Both the Centre and its many spin-offs are involved in the annual anti-Semitic Quds demonstrations in Berlin, whose participants call for the destruction of Israel.

Outside these large associations there is a smaller one, the Ahmadiyya Muslim Jamaat, which is not accepted by many Sunnis but plays an important role as a cooperation partner of the state. The Ahmadiyah Muslim Jamaat is the only Muslim association that is recognised as a full religious organisation by the German state. However, the organisation propagates a rigid gender segregation, the subordination of women, and considers the caliphate the only true Islamic order.

Although these groups differ from one another in many ways, they are linked by a fundamentalist understanding of Islam. While progressive Muslims either interpret the religious texts in their historical context or by means of other hermeneutical methods, fundamentalists insist on a literal interpretation. This is, of course, problematic because some verses are anti-Semitic or legitimise violence whereas others justify discrimination against women as God's will. Fundamentalism does not necessarily need to include a political plan for action. There are isolated communities that completely submit to religious regulations but do not develop any ambitions to change society. To the vast majority of Islamic fundamentalists, however, such self-centredness does not apply. Their agenda is usually not about a community order in which the pious live among their own kind according to their own rules, but about a social order, that is, about reshaping societies on the basis of Islamic principles. The efforts are aimed at the establishment of an order that is God's will in the Islamic sense, and in concrete terms the rule of Islam. In this sense, we are dealing with an ideology of domination that religiously defines the desired normative order in a fundamentalist framework. As a rule, this does not mean that fundamentalists want to establish a caliphate, as this would thwart the differences among them. Rather, it is about enforcing norms taken from a fundamentalist understanding of Islam. These norms are set absolutely because they are supposed to have been issued by God, and they are enforced by all means.

If Islamist actors try to achieve their goals in a peaceful way, we speak of a legalistic political Islam. If they choose the means of violence, then it is jihadism or Islamist terrorism. In contrast to what is proclaimed by some catalogues of measures for the deradicalisation or the prevention of extremism, there is no categorical, but primarily a strategic, and sometimes a moral, difference between the two varieties of political Islam. Many jihadists came from the Muslim Brotherhood; in other contexts there are alliances between legalistic and jihadist forces. This is the case, for example, in Turkey under President Erdogan, who always kept the border to Syria open for jihadist travel and invariably used jihadist auxiliaries in his wars against the Syrian Kurds. It is thus not surprising that DİTİB, which he controls, tries legalistically to enforce Islamic norms in schools in Germany, while at the same time having martyr sermons held in its mosques and encouraging children to engage in military performances, which are then framed as holy wars.

In recent years, the aforementioned organisations of political Islam have made many attempts to implement Islamic norms in Germany. The result can be seen in schools, for example, where some Muslim parents prohibit their children from taking part in co-educational swimming, sports classes and school trips. Girls in elementary schools already refuse to sit next to boys and wear a headscarf because they have been taught that otherwise they would end up in hell fire after death. Religious bullying is increasing. It affects non-Muslim children who are insulted as infidels, but also Muslim children who do not submit to the rules of the game that are proclaimed in the mosques. The pressure to fast during Ramadan, to go to the mosque on Friday and not to make friends with non-Muslim classmates is steadily growing. Teachers complain about insults and lack of respect, and fear complaints when visiting churches or taking part in Christian celebrations. In many school canteens pork is no longer served, and in some schools Muslim parents have enforced that meat is obtained solely from animals butchered in accordance with Islam. This development leads to permanent conflict as well as permanent attempts to undermine the state's principle of neutrality. Headscarf-wearing women, who often turned out to be Muslim Association officials, repeatedly invoked their supposed right to take on government representation tasks with a visible sign of their religious creed. We are even witnessing an increase of women who want to take part in university seminars or even take exams with facial veils. Whenever the targeted enforcement of Islamic norms is met with resistance, the representatives of political Islam try to silence their opponents with the accusation of Islamophobia or anti-Muslim racism.

6 Progressive Muslims

The strongest voices against political Islam are currently coming from progressive Muslims and critical intellectuals of Muslim origin. I would like to divide this group into three categories: 1) Sufi orders; 2) secular organisations and liberal Islamic projects; and 3) progressive theologies. Not all Sufis are progressive, but some are. One of their progressive organisations is the Federation of Muslim Boy and Girl Scouts of Germany. The founder, Fouad Hartit, likes to say that he does not consider learning the Qur'an a sufficient pastime for young Muslims. To him, scouting seems more suitable for opening up a world of experience, having fun, mastering challenges, and assuming a responsibility for oneself and others. According to Hartit, young Muslims should show that they are ordinary Germans who have the same needs as other young people, that they are not marginalised but live right in the heart of society, and that they identify with this country.

Among the liberal initiatives I would like to mention the Ibn Rush-Goethe Mosque, founded in 2017 by Seyran Ateş. In this mosque, women hold Friday sermons, wearing a headscarf is not necessary, gays and non-Muslims are expressly invited. A group founded in 2018, which sees itself primarily as a catalyst for the Islam debate in Germany, is the initiative of secular Islam, which already has a regional organisation in the federal state of Rhineland-Palatinate and another in Hamburg. Some secular Muslims have the status of public intellectuals. One of these is the Israeli-born Arab psychologist Ahmad Mansour, who works with Muslim youths and has developed some innovative concepts for extremism prevention. Public intellectuals also include sociologist Necla Kelek, a profound critic of patriarchal-Islamic family structures, and political science scholar Hamed Abdel-Samad who writes about the legitimisation of violence in the Qur'an and Sunnah. The tragedy of liberal Muslims is that they have to live with denunciations and insults, and have little influence on the mixed communities. Some are intimidated by death threats. When Seyran Ateş opened her mosque, she received over 100 death threats by e-mail during the first night. The Turkish religion authority Diyanet accused her of undermining and destroying Islam and denounced her team as puppets of Fethullah Gülen, and the Egyptian Fatwa Office rated the founding of the Ibn Rushd-Goethe Mosque as an attack on the religion of Islam. Seyran Ateş, Ahmad Mansur and Hamed Abdel-Samad have to live with police protection.

7 The German Debate on Islam and Official Islam Politics

How can Islamic politics in Germany continue under these conditions? I have already mentioned that many measures did not have the expected effect. Let us take the Islamic studies centres at state universities as an example. Many millions of euros have been invested in filling professorships and equipping institutes.

Linked to this was the expectation that a modern Islamic theology would develop that could counterbalance the fundamentalist orientation of the Islamist associations. However, these centres had a birth defect, so to speak. They were given advisory boards to which representatives of the aforementioned Islamist organisations were appointed. These advisory boards decide on curricula and appointments and can exert their influence if a professor does not meet their expectations. Using the example of the Münsteran professor Mouhanad Khorchide I will illustrate what this means for progressive Muslims. In 2014, Khorchide published a monograph entitled *Islam is Mercy*, which provoked fierce opposition by the large Turkish associations. The idea of a God who is primarily loving, the repudiation of certain concepts such as hell, as well as the historicisation of both the Qur'an and the Islamic traditions were condemned by the representatives of the associations as being heretical aberrations. The council condemned Khorchide for straying from the alleged right path, and demanded the dismissal of the professor on the grounds that he is, in their opinion, no longer a true Muslim. However, the Federal Government demonstratively supported Khorchide and honoured him with a visit by the Federal President when the debate had reached its peak. The second problem is that liberal professors are rejected and bullied by students. This has created pressure to conform, and at the moment no one but Khorchide seems to dare to come up with ideas that contradict fundamentalist orthodoxy. The third problem concerns the lack of acceptance of the institutes by representatives of associations and mosque communities. Academic Islamic institutes are conceived as institutions of higher learning that train not only future scholars of Islam but also imams and school teachers of the Islamic religion. However, the organisations of political Islam refuse to hire personal from the state universities. Therefore, only school teaching remains as a career perspective beyond science. I have already mentioned that confessional religious education was launched in several federal states. However, in Hesse, where that programme was most advanced, cooperation with DİTİB was discontinued in April 2020 after years of criticism and on the basis of various scholarly reports complaining about the dependency of DİTİB on the Turkish government. In other federal states, too, there is currently no agreement on how to proceed. The major Islamic organisations are not only suspected of being anti-democratic but also lack recognition as religious communities. This recognition has been requested by DİTİB, Millî Görüs and the Central Council of Muslims. So far, their attempts have failed due to court rulings and doubts as to whether they are religious or rather political groups. Foreign dependency is also viewed critically.

What about state contracts with Islamist organisations? After all, there are contracts and agreements between politics and Islamist organisations, but they are criticised by sceptics of all political parties. Points of criticism are the fundamentalist orientation of the Islamic associations, their proximity to extremists, and their anti-liberal ideology. A debate has just begun about the state contracts of the federal state of Hamburg with DİTİB and the Islamic Centre Hamburg. The Christian Democratic Union of Germany (CDU) calls for termination of the contracts and is considering a ban on the Islamic Centre Hamburg because of its closeness to the banned Hezbollah and anti-Semitic activities. The Green Party and the Social Democrats, on the other hand, want to continue the cooperation. An essential core of the problem is that politicians apply the state church-law of the Weimar Constitution when they enter into cooperation with Muslims. However, it is Christian churches that are at the centre of that law. If that model is applied to Islamic organisations, it always profits the organisations of political Islam, as they are the only ones that can come up with associations that have many thousands of members. Secular Muslims are naturally not involved in religious organisations but rather in trade unions, parents' councils or sports clubs. They will therefore not be involved. Progressive and liberal Muslims, on the other hand, are under great pressure and their representatives' lives are at risk, so it is hardly to be expected that many Muslims will openly join their ranks. The result is that political Islam is increasingly dominating the stage of state Islam policy. Its main advantage is its high degree of organisation and a group of well-trained functionaries who claim authority to interpret Islam and are perceived as the legitimate representatives of all Muslims in Germany.

This causes several dilemmas. 1) The majority of Muslims or citizens with a Muslim background in Germany have no access to politics or to public funds that can be used to finance projects; 2) an Islamist minority is subsidised by the state and dominates the image of Islam in Germany; 3) since most Germans' image of Islam is shaped by the Islamists, Islam has a bad reputation. The majority of the population does not believe that it is compatible with European values; 4) Islamist terrorist attacks and disputes over Islamic norms trigger a feeling of danger, which is associated with Islam, in the population; 5) these fears are an important basis for right-wing extremist mobilisations; 6) right-wing radicalism and Islamism mutually reinforce each other and lead to a tense security situation; 7) instead of the immigration society growing together, there are more divisions and the development of disintegrative, segregated milieus.

So far, no solution is emerging that would be suitable to pacify the situation. The debate about Islam in Germany will thus continue in the future.

Kristina Stoeckl
Europe's New Religious Conflicts: Russian Orthodoxy, American Christian Conservatives and the Emergence of a European Populist Christian Right-Wing

The fall of the Berlin Wall thirty years ago marked the end of one era and the beginning of a new one. The end of the Cold War, the end of the division of Europe between a communist East and a capitalist West, promised social and political change. It promised the dawn of an open society, oriented towards individual human rights and democratic institutions, a free market and free academia.

Twenty years later, many achievements have been made, but also many setbacks have materialised. In 2020, the Central European University moved from Budapest to Vienna, because laws passed by the right-wing populist Hungarian government made it impossible for it to stay there. Poland has embarked on a judicial reform that the European Commission considers to be a violation of EU rules. In Bulgaria, the Constitutional Court has refused to ratify the Istanbul Convention, a Council of Europe document on gender-based violence. Russia adopted a constitution that will allow it to ignore the European Convention on Human Rights. Three decades after the end of the Cold War, Europe appears torn and divided again, only in different ways from in the past. "The End of history",[1] as Francis Fukuyama called the vision of the global triumph of a liberal order after the end of the Cold War, has not taken place. Much malice has been poured over the thesis of the end of history. A crude philosophy of history, a Hegelian vision, haunted, as Jacques Derrida judged, by "the specters of Marx".[2] A vision that ignored the dark side of liberalism, the material inequality in capitalism, injustice, racism, and sexism, such was the criticism waged against "The End of History". The theory that an open society and liberalism will inevitably prevail has always been controversial, and it is now – after the global economic and debt crisis, after the rise of right-wing populist politicians on all continents – over and done with. However, I do not want to speak about the liberal order ironically. Instead, I seek to understand, from the vantage point of *the end* of the end of the Cold War, in which condition liberal

---

1 F. Fukuyama, "The End of History?", *The National Interest* 16 (1989): 3–18.
2 J. Derrida, *Spectres de Marx: l'État de la dette, le travail du deuil et la nouvelle Internationale* (Paris: Galilée, 1993); English translation: *Specters of Marx: The State of the Debt, the Work of Mourning and the New International* (New York/London: Routledge, 1994).

democratic values are in Europe and in the world today. By liberal democratic values, I mean: democratic values (the idea that power in a state comes from the people) coupled with guarantees for minorities (even a democratic majority cannot oppress minorities in its midst) and limited state sovereignty (the state is bound by treaties to supranational human rights standards). Why are these liberal political values going through a crisis today?

There are many avenues one could take to answer this question. From a political economy perspective, we could point to how rising social inequalities raise questions about the liberal democratic social contract. From a political perspective, we could identify controversies over migration and the rise of populism as the main important factor in this crisis. The perspective I develop in this essay is that of a political sociology of religions. I want to consider the crisis of the liberal democratic order through the lens of the religion-society-politics triangle. What does this lens reveal about our political situation today? Three theoretical perspectives are helpful here.

First, secularisation: the secularisation thesis states that traditional religions are losing importance in modern societies, that they are moving out of public life and politics into the private sphere, and that fewer and fewer people are practising a religion (in the classical formulation of Peter Berger).[3] The question as to whether secularisation makes religions disappear or not, has already filled many book-shelves. But in a way, it is a wrongly posed question. It is more interesting to ask how secularisation *changes* religions. That secularisation *does* change religions is undeniable. Churches and religious communities first reacted to secularisation defensively, and then, after the Second World War – as the Catholic Church did in the course of the Second Vatican Council – with a change of attitude: the Catholic and Protestant churches have largely accepted that their status has changed from being a power that dictates the social and political order of a society to being *one* formative force among others.[4] To the same extent that religions have acquired the status of one association among others, their relationship to politics has also changed. Where previously religion preceded political decisions, religion now becomes one of the factors influencing politics. As a consequence, a paradoxical shift within modern religions takes place: while religions as a practice of faith under conditions of secular modernity have become more diverse and pluralistic, religions as institutions within the state – in the framework of national legisla-

---

[3] P.L. Berger, *The Sacred Canopy: Elements of a Sociological Theory of Religion* (New York: Doubleday, 1967).

[4] J. Casanova, "Global Religious and Secular Dynamics. The Modern System of Classification", *Religion and Politics* 1/1 (2019): 1–74.

tions – have become more uniform and more legalised. Olivier Roy speaks in this context of a "formatting of religion" according to the rules of the constitutional state.[5]

Second: functional theories of religion, as in Robert Bellah's well-known concept of civil religion, assume that in modern societies religion continues to have a cultural and community-building effect, even if it is no longer recognisable as such.[6] From this perspective, the profane values and symbols of a society can become 'sacred', not for theological or religious reasons, but – ultimately – for sociological and political reasons. A different interpretation is put forward by Jocelyne Cesari drawing on Jean-Jacques Rousseau's original take on *religion civile*. There, civil religion means "a state-centred project aimed at securing the loyalties of citizens through rituals and symbols".[7] Civil religion in this sense is a state-centred religion, and not – or not first and foremost – a system of shared beliefs. The implication of civil religion as a state-centred religion is that the religious tradition in question and the state are mutually constitutive, that they depend on each other and that they are transformed by their relationship.

In order to illustrate the two theoretical perspectives, let me add two examples. Both are taken from my current research, the "Postsecular Conflicts" research project, which is concerned with the transnational and interdenominational dynamics of value conflicts and their protagonists, in particular with the role of one protagonist that could be called a newcomer to the global culture wars: Russia and the Russian Orthodox Church.[8]

In the thirty years since the end of the Cold War, the Russian Orthodox Church has gradually moved from being one religion in the Russian Federation to becoming the provider of a new civil religion for the Russian state. An architectural expression of this idea can be visited on the outskirts of Moscow, where the Moscow Patriarchate and the Russian Ministry of Defence have built a monumental cathedral to the Russian Armed Forces. The cathedral made headlines in spring 2020 when plans to install an art work representing Vladimir Putin in the church became

---

[5] O. Roy, "Rethinking the Place of Religion in European Secularized Societies: The Need for More Open Societies", Conclusion of Research Project ReligioWest, Robert Schuman Centre for Advanced Studies, European University Institute, March 2016, available at http://cadmus.eui.eu/handle/1814/40305 (accessed 12 January 2021).
[6] R.N. Bellah, *The Broken Covenant: American Civil Religion in a Time of Trial* (New York: Seabury, 1975).
[7] J. Cesari, *What is Political Islam?* (Boulder: Lynne Rienner, 2018), 193.
[8] Visit the website here: https://www.uibk.ac.at/projects/postsecular-conflicts/ (accessed 12 January 2021).

public. The plan did not materialise in the end, but, in any case, the building itself is the visual expression of Russia's new civil religion.[9]

From the perspective of civil religion as a state-centred religion, a commitment to liberal political values is not obvious: democracy, the idea that power in the state emanates from the people, may still be valid from this perspective, but it is actually irrelevant, because if society and politics are equally permeated by religion, democratic negotiation is no longer needed. There is no need for liberal minority rights at all, but only – the current slogan of the Russian government and the Moscow Patriarchate in unison – for "traditional values".[10] In Russia, these traditional values are decreed by state laws: the ban on homosexual propaganda, the ban on violating religious feelings, the ban on swearwords in theatre and film – in recent years the Kremlin has implemented many laws that shape society according to the canon of traditional values.

From the secularisation perspective, the significance of liberal political values is completely different. Here, religion is seen as inwardly differentiated and, at its external border, where it meets the secular state, as legally defined. It is a part of civil society *vis-à-vis* the state and state institutions. Religion is therefore dependent on pluralistic, liberal democratic values, if only for its own survival. Religion should become, out of pure logic, a protector of these pluralistic, liberal democratic values.

Even for this last perspective one can find an example from the Russian Orthodox context. In September 2019, more than 170 priests of the Russian Orthodox Church published an open letter calling for the release of young demonstrators who had been arrested in August during peaceful street protests against the Moscow city government. During the protest marches, demonstrators had repeatedly sought – and found – shelter from police in churches in downtown Moscow. With this letter, the priests sent a signal that the Russian Orthodox Church was not only a pillar of the Russian state, but could also be an opponent, standing on the side of civil protests for free elections. What was particularly interesting about this protest of the priests was that in their letter they referred to the legacy of the well-known dissident priest of the Soviet era, Alexander Men.

There can also be a third perspective on the relationship between religion, society and politics, the perspective of culture wars. *Culture Wars* is an analysis

---

[9] For a more detailed argument, see K. Stoeckl, "Russian Orthodoxy and Secularism", *Religion and Politics* 1/2 (2020): 1–75, on pp. 49–56.
[10] See A. Agadjanian, "Tradition, Morality and Community: Elaborating Orthodox Identity in Putin's Russia", *Religion, State and Society* 45/1 (2017): 39–60; E. Stepanova, "'The Spiritual and Moral Foundations of Civilization in Every Nation for Thousands of Years': The Traditional Values Discourse in Russia", *Politics, Religion and Ideology* 16/2–3 (2015): 119–136.

by the American sociologist James Hunter, who uses it to describe the conflicts between progressive and conservative groups in the United States on issues such as abortion and homosexuality.[11] These moral conflicts, Hunter noted, have polarised American society for decades, and they polarise religious communities in particular. Religious market theory supports this analysis. It describes religions as competitors in a free market of world views, where extreme, strong messages – extremely conservative or extremely progressive – have competitive advantages over moderate messages. The moderate, large churches lose believers, the radical religious communities gain them.[12] In this situation, ideological differences become more important than confessional ones. The culture wars lead to interdenominational coalitions and mobilisation. From the culture wars perspective, the religion-society-politics triangle looks different again. Culture wars are battles over what stands at the centre of this trial. It is not so much democracy that is under attack, but the added term *liberal*: conservatives generally reject the idea that the democratic state actively protects all minorities from discrimination as a form of relativism. Liberals, likewise, find it difficult to accept that liberal democratic minority rights may end up to the benefit of illiberal lifestyles – a topic recently explored by Susanna Mancini and Michel Rosenfeld in the volume *The Conscience Wars*.[13]

That the culture wars described by Hunter in 1991 have become a global phenomenon is not a novelty. What is relatively new is that Russia and the Russian Orthodox Church have become active players in the global culture wars.[14] In the thirty years since the end of the Cold War, the Russian Orthodox Church is itself being shaped by the culture war dynamics, with the result that today the Russian Orthodox discourse on traditional values mirrors the topics, patterns and strategies of Christian Right groups in the West. American Christian Right groups actively promoted conservative family values and traditional gender roles in the early years after Perestroika.[15] Their Cold War anti-leftism and anti-liberalism resonated with the disillusionment felt by many Russians with regard to the Soviet past and to the chaotic transition to market liberalism of the 1990s. Scholars and observers have, for the most part, been interested in the question as to how post-Communist soci-

---

11 J.D. Hunter, *Culture Wars: The Struggle to Define America* (New York: Basic Books, 1991).
12 R. Finke/R. Stark, "Religious Choice and Competition", *American Sociological Review* 63/5 (1998): 761–766.
13 S. Mancini/M. Rosenfeld (ed.), *The Conscience Wars: Rethinking the Balance between Religion and Equality* (Cambridge: Cambridge University Press, 2018).
14 See K. Stoeckl/D. Uzlaner (ed.), *Postsecular Conflicts: Debating Tradition in Russia and the United States* (Innsbruck: Innsbruck University Press, 2020).
15 P.L. Glanzer, *The Quest for Russia's Soul: Evangelicals and Moral Education in Post-Communist Russia* (Waco, TX: Baylor University Press, 2002).

eties 'learnt' about democracy, liberalism, and the advantages of an open society. What such a perspective overlooked (or downplayed due to an intrinsic bias) were the existing tensions within the Western social order described by Hunter as "culture wars". Illiberal, traditionalist and social conservative ideas were also part of the Western exportation of ideas to post-Soviet Russia, and they became an important source for contemporary Russian conservatism.[16]

The engagement of Russian Orthodoxy on the frontlines of the global culture wars can be interpreted as an indicator of an increasing 'marketisation' of religion. In his book *Holy Ignorance*,[17] Olivier Roy has made the argument that present-day conservative religious tendencies are not the fruit of a (re-)rooting of religions in traditional societies, but instead the result of a global diffusion of 'markers' of religious conservatism that owe little to traditional concerns and practices and more to modern political dynamics. "No to abortion" and "no to same-sex marriage" are the global markers of religious conservatism for Protestant Evangelicals in the United States and in Brazil, for conservative Catholics in France and Honduras, and for Orthodox traditionalists alike.

Russian anti-liberalism is attractive to conservative Christians in the West, who resent the liberal and secular character of their own societies. This is particularly true in some of the new member states of the European Union, who have recently experienced a political right-turn. The conservative resentment over rapidly changing societies is frequently wedded to a general opposition to the European Union and Brussel's control over national politics. This explains why some right-wing parties in Europe have not only adopted the anti-liberal rhetoric of traditional values, but have also looked to Putin's Russia for a model of authoritarian government.[18] However, in the United States, too, conservative Christians have been attracted to Russian Orthodoxy as a stronghold of traditional values, as is demonstrated in the ethnographic work on conversions to Russian Orthodoxy by Sarah Riccardi-Swartz.[19]

---

[16] This connection is explored in more detail in Stoeckl/Uzlaner (ed.), *Postsecular Conflicts*. See also M. Suslov/D. Uzlaner (ed.), *Contemporary Russian Conservatism: Problems, Paradoxes, and Perspectives* (Leiden: Brill, 2019).

[17] O. Roy, *Holy Ignorance: When Religion and Culture Diverge* (New York: Columbia University Press, 2009).

[18] M. Laruelle (ed.), *Entangled Far Rights: A Russian-European Intellectual Romance in the Twentieth Century* (Pittsburgh: Pittsburgh University Press, 2018) and M. Laruelle, "Mirror Games?: Ideological Resonances between Russian and US Radical Conservatism", in Suslov/Uzlaner (ed.), *Contemporary Russian Conservatism*, 177–204.

[19] S. Riccardi-Swartz, "American Conversions to Russian Orthodoxy Amid the Global Culture Wars", *Berkley Center Blog "The Culture Wars Today"*, 18 December 2019, available at https://

For conservatives in the West and in the Global South, Russia under Vladimir Putin has become an attractive partner against liberal values and against an international human rights regime that is frequently perceived as "too liberal".[20] Scholars have usually interpreted the Russian Orthodox Church's international value-based agenda as an instrument of Russian soft power and foreign policy.[21] I argue, instead, that we need to focus on the Russian Orthodox Church as a moral norm entrepreneur in its own right. The Moscow Patriarchate has consistently acted as a moral conservative agent at the international level in different institutional forums since 2008; the Moscow Patriarchate and the Russian state have co-created and co-defined a Russian leadership role in the promotion of traditional values against the liberal international human rights regime, and hence Russia has become a key-player in the global culture wars. The Russian Orthodox Church today is as global as it is national. It is part of a worldwide religious market in which its appeal lies precisely in being considered a particularly conservative church. In this situation, the boundaries between the Russian Orthodox Church and the Russian state are blurred.

The fascination with Russia and traditional values as a bulwark against liberalism is evident not only among conservative Christians in the United States and in the new member states of the European Union. It can also be observed among the populist right in Western Europe. One example was the World Congress of Families, which took place in Verona in March 2019. The event was organised by the American International Organization for the Family (IOF) and the Italian NGO Pro Vita e Famiglia, and it was supported by the Italian League Party, which was in government at the time. It was met by impressive street mobilisation on the part of feminist and women's rights groups, such as the NGO Non una di meno, who were joined by activists from other parts of Europe. Verona provided a glimpse of the reality of global culture wars. Why – one may ask – has the Italian League – which worshipped the waters of the river Po under its founder Umberto Bossi – turned into a defender of traditional Christian values? Why does its leader, Matteo Salvini, not miss a single opportunity to present himself with a crucifix or rosary in his hand? The answer is not only that the League is exploiting Christianity against

---

berkleycenter.georgetown.edu/responses/american-conversions-to-russian-orthodoxy-amid-the-global-culture-wars (accessed 12 January 2021).
20 C. McCrudden, "Human Rights, Southern Voices, and 'Traditional Values' at the United Nations", *University of Michigan Public Law Research Paper* 419 (2014), available at http://ssrn.com/abstract=2474241 (accessed 12 January 2021).
21 A. Curanović, "The Guardians of Traditional Values: Russia and the Russian Orthodox Church in the Quest for Status", in M. Barnett *et al.* (ed.), *Faith, Freedom and Foreign Policy: Challenges for the Transatlantic Community* (Washington: Transatlantic Academy, 2015), 191–212.

Islam and against immigration, although this is one part of the answer. The answer is that conservative family values have become a global currency for actors on the right who want to oppose liberal democratic values and supranational human rights.

In the "Postsecular Conflicts" research project and our publications we have explored in considerable detail the ways in which, during the early 1990s, the American Christian Right exported its ideas to Russia and to the Russian Orthodox Church. Scholars of Russian Orthodoxy – and I do not exclude myself here – have for a long time overlooked these ties and influences because the emergence of Orthodoxy as Russia's new civil religion appeared more important or more relevant. In reality, however, the moral conservative norm of mobilisation against same-sex marriage, against abortion, and against LGBTQ-rights has united Christian conservatives from the United States, Europe and Russia. As Evangelicals, Catholics and Orthodox actors from different countries form transnational and interdenominational coalitions against liberal values, they reshape the presence of religion in national political and public debates. They challenge established religion-state relations in different national contexts, and also the leadership of their churches.

The globalising culture wars and the new role of Russia as a promotor of conservative, traditional Christian values gives rise to a new type of religious conflict in Europe, which is no longer between the different confessions and no longer between the religious and secular, but over the very meaning of Christianity in Europe. At first I asked the question why the expectations of an open society were disappointed after the end of the Cold War. Why are liberal political values going through a crisis today? And what role does religion play in this crisis? I think that we have now taken one step further towards answering this question. Actually, the question why liberal political values are contested today is misplaced. They have always been the subject of criticism, and that is normal in a pluralistic society with different views of what constitutes a good life. Religion is a legitimate source of such views. But the questions as to how liberal democratic values have become controversial today, who is making them controversial, and by what means – these are questions that we as scholars should and can answer. The triangle religion-society-politics and the lens of Russian Orthodoxy has opened up new perspectives on the panorama of Europe's new religious conflicts.

Notes on Contributors

Herman J. Selderhuis is Rector of the Theological University of Apeldoorn, where he holds the Chair of Church History and Church Polity, is President of the Reformation Research Consortium (RefoRC), and was President of the European Academy of Religion (2019-2020). His most recent publications are: "Martin Luther in the Netherlands", in *Reformation and Renaissance Review* (21/2, 2019, 142-153); "Konfessionelle Kulturen und normative Konkurrenzen – Divergenzen, Karikaturen und normative Konkurrenzen", in Klaus Fitschen *et al.* (ed.), *Kulturelle Wirkungen der Reformation / Cultural Impact of the Reformation* (Evangelische Verlagsanstalt, 2019, 19-31); "'Schepken Christy' in fremdem Hafen. Die Bedeutung Emdens für den Niederländischen Calvinismus", in Frank van der Pol (ed.), *The Doctrine of Election in Reformed Perspective: Historical and Theological Investigations of the Synod of Dort 1618-1619* (Vandenhoeck & Ruprecht, 2018, 13-22).

R. Scott Appleby is the Marilyn Keough Dean of Notre Dame's Keough School of Global Affairs. A professor of History at Notre Dame, he is a scholar of Global Religion who has been a member of Notre Dame's faculty since 1994. He graduated from Notre Dame in 1978 and received M.A. and Ph.D. degrees in History from the University of Chicago. From 2000 to 2014, he served as the Regan Director of the Kroc Institute for International Peace Studies. Appleby co-directs, with Ebrahim Moosa and Atalia Omer, "Contending Modernities", a major multi-year project to examine the interaction among Catholic, Muslim, and secular forces in the modern world. Appleby is the author or editor of fifteen books, including the volumes of *The Fundamentalism Project* (University of Chicago Press, 1991–1995) co-edited with Martin E. Marty and *The Ambivalence of the Sacred: Religion, Violence and Reconciliation* (Rowman and Littlefield, 2000). Most recently, Appleby co-edited with Atalia Omer *The Oxford Handbook of Religion, Conflict and Peacebuilding* (Oxford University Press, 2019). He also serves as head editor of the Oxford University Press series "Studies in Strategic Peacebuilding." A fellow of the American Academy of Arts and Sciences and of the American Academy of Political and Social Sciences, Appleby is the recipient of four honorary doctorates, from Fordham University, Scranton University, St. John's University (Collegeville, Minnesota) and Saint Xavier University (Chicago).

Archimandrite **Cyril Hovorun** is professor in Ecclesiology, International Relations and Ecumenism at the Sankt Ignatios College, University College Stockholm, and a director of the Huffington Ecumenical Institute at Loyola Marymount University in Los Angeles. A graduate of the Theological Academy in Kyiv and National University in Athens, he accomplished his doctoral studies at Durham University. He was a Chairman of the Department for External Church Relations of the Ukrainian Orthodox Church, First Deputy Chairman of the Educational Committee of the Russian Orthodox Church, and later a research fellow at Yale and Columbia Universities. Among the books that he has published are: *Eastern Christianity in Its Texts* (Bloomsbury, 2022); *Political Orthodoxies: The Unorthodoxies of the Church Coerced* (Fortress, 2018); *Scaffolds of the Church: Towards Poststructural Ecclesiology* (Cascade, 2017); *Meta-Ecclesiology, Chronicles on Church Awareness* (Palgrave Macmillan, 2015); *Will, Action and Freedom: Christological Controversies in the Seventh Century* (Brill, 2008).

Susanne Schröter is professor of Social and Cultural Anthropology at the Goethe University in Frankfurt and Director of the Frankfurt Research Center on Global Islam. She previously taught at Yale University, the Universities of Mainz and Trier and held the Chair of Southeast Asian Studies at the University of Passau. She regularly advises political institutions and civil society organisations on questions of extremism prevention, integration and the politics of Islam. In Frankfurt, Susanne

Schröter is head of a long-term project on the transformation of normative orders in the Islamic world. Her publications include: *Christianity in Indonesia: Perspectives of Power* (Lit, 2010); *Gender and Islam in Southeast Asia: Women's Rights Movements, Religious Resurgence and Local Traditions* (Brill, 2013); and "Islamic Feminism: National and Transnational Dimensions", in J. Cesari/J. Casanova (ed.), *Islam, Gender and Democracy in Comparative Perspective* (Oxford University Press, 2017, 115–138). The following books have recently appeared in the German language: *"Gott näher als der eigenen Halsschlagader": Fromme Muslime in Deutschland* (Campus, 2016); *Normenkonflikte in pluralistischen Gesellschaften* (Campus, 2017); and *Politischer Islam: Stresstest für Deutschland* (Gütersloher Verlagshaus, 2019).

Kristina Stoeckl is professor of Sociology at LUISS Rome. From 2015 until 2023 she worked at the Department of Sociology of the University of Innsbruck and was principal investigator of the European Research Council funded project "Postsecular Conflicts" (2016–2022). She holds a Ph.D. from the European University Institute (Florence) and in the past has held research and teaching positions at the University of Rome Tor Vergata, the University of Vienna, the Central European University, the Robert Schumann Center for Advanced Studies, and the Institute for Human Sciences IWM (Vienna). Her research areas are sociology of religion and social and political theory, with a focus on Orthodox Christianity, religion-state relations in Russia and problems of political liberalism and religion. After her monograph *The Russian Orthodox Church and Human Rights* (Routledge, 2014), she has recently published (together with Dmitry Uzlaner) *Moralist International. Russia in the Global Culture Wars* (Fordham 2022).

Index of Names

Abdel-Samad, Hamed 50
Al-Husayni, Muhammad Amin 42
Arendt, Hannah 21, 40
Arius 23
Aron, Raymond 20–21, 38
Ateş, Seyran 50
Augustus II the Strong 50
Bellah, Robert 55
Çelebi, Mehmet Alparslan 47
Çelebi, Musa Serdar 47
Cesari, Jocelyne 55
Clodius, Johann Christian 42
Constantine 21–22, 31
Cyril of Alexandria 30
Derrida, Jacques 53
Eusebius of Caesarea 21–24
Erbakan, Necmettin 46
Erdoğan, Recep Tayyip 46, 49
Fleischer, Heinrich Leberecht 42
Friedrich, Hans-Peter 43
Fukuyama, Francis 53
Gauck, Joachim 43
Geréby, György 18
Goethe, Johann Wolfgang von 42
Gregory of Nazianzus 19–20
Grimm, Fatima 47
Hartit, Fouad 50
Heraclius 30
Himmler, Heinrich 42
Hitler, Adolf 17, 34–36
Hunter, James 57–58
Jenkins, Jerry B. 11
Jesus Christ 7, 11–13, 22, 26–27, 29–31, 39
John Chrysostom 30
Jones, Bob 11
Justinian 29–30

Kantorowicz, Ernst 25–28
Kaplan, Cemaleddin 46
Kaplan, Metin 46
Kelek, Necla 50
Khomeini 14
Khorchide, Mouhanad 51
LaHaye, Tim 11
Ljotić, Dimitrije 34
Mansour, Ahmad 50
Marcus Terentius Varro 17
Mazyek, Aiman 47
Mancini, Susanna 57
Men, Alexander 56
Moltmann, Jürgen 39
Muhammad 42, 45
Mussolini, Benito 34
Nestorius 31
Nilus, Sergei 36,
Nöldeke, Theodor 42
Norman Anonymous 26–27
Oppenheim, Max von 42
Peterson, Erik 17–21, 23, 25–26, 38–40
Pseudo-Dionysius 25
Putin, Vladimir 55, 58–59
Riccardi-Swartz, Sarah 58
Rosenfeld, Michel 57
Rousseau, Jean-Jacques 55
Roy, Olivier 55, 58
Salvini, Matteo 59
Schäuble, Wolfgang 44
Schmitt, Carl 17–18, 20–22, 24, 25, 38
Sivan, Emmanuel 6
Soloveitchik, Haym 15
Veer, Peter van der 12
Velimirović, Nikolaj 34, 37
Wulff, Christian 43

www.ingramcontent.com/pod-product-compliance
Lightning Source LLC
Chambersburg PA
CBHW020131010526

44115CB00008B/1068